The Standard for
ORGANIZATIONAL PROJECT
MANAGEMENT (OPM)

Library of Congress Cataloging-in-Publication Data

Title: The standard for organizational project management (OPM).

Description: Newtown Square, PA : Project Management Institute, 2018. |
    Includes bibliographical references and index.
Identifiers: LCCN 2018018297 (print) | LCCN 2018020060 (ebook) | ISBN
    9781628255546 (ePUB) | ISBN 9781628255553 (kindle) | ISBN 9781628255560
    (Web PDF) | ISBN 9781628252002 (paperback)
Subjects: LCSH: Project management. | Project management–Standards. | BISAC:
    BUSINESS & ECONOMICS / Project Management.
Classification: LCC HD69.P75 (ebook) | LCC HD69.P75 S73 2018 (print) | DDC
    658.4/04–dc23
LC record available at https://lccn.loc.gov/2018018297

ISBN: 978-1-62825-200-2

Published by:
    Project Management Institute, Inc.
    18 Campus Boulevard
    Newtown Square, Pennsylvania 19073-3299
    USA Phone +1 610-356-4600
    Email: customercare@pmi.org
    Website: www.PMI.org

To place a Trade Order or for pricing information, please contact Independent Publishers Group:
    Independent Publishers Group
    Order Department
    814 North Franklin Street
    Chicago, IL 60610 USA
    Phone: +1 800-888-4741
    Fax: +1 312-337-5985
    Email: orders@ipgbook.com (For orders only)

10 9 8 7 6 5 4 3

NOTICE

The Project Management Institute, Inc. (PMI) standards and guideline publications, of which the document contained herein is one, are developed through a voluntary consensus standards development process. This process brings together volunteers and/or seeks out the views of persons who have an interest in the topic covered by this publication. While PMI administers the process and establishes rules to promote fairness in the development of consensus, it does not write the document and it does not independently test, evaluate, or verify the accuracy or completeness of any information or the soundness of any judgments contained in its standards and guideline publications.

PMI disclaims liability for any personal injury, property or other damages of any nature whatsoever, whether special, indirect, consequential or compensatory, directly or indirectly resulting from the publication, use of application, or reliance on this document. PMI disclaims and makes no guaranty or warranty, expressed or implied, as to the accuracy or completeness of any information published herein, and disclaims and makes no warranty that the information in this document will fulfill any of your particular purposes or needs. PMI does not undertake to guarantee the performance of any individual manufacturer or seller's products or services by virtue of this standard or guide.

In publishing and making this document available, PMI is not undertaking to render professional or other services for or on behalf of any person or entity, nor is PMI undertaking to perform any duty owed by any person or entity to someone else. Anyone using this document should rely on his or her own independent judgment or, as appropriate, seek the advice of a competent professional in determining the exercise of reasonable care in any given circumstances. Information and other standards on the topic covered by this publication may be available from other sources, which the user may wish to consult for additional views or information not covered by this publication.

PMI has no power, nor does it undertake to police or enforce compliance with the contents of this document. PMI does not certify, test, or inspect products, designs, or installations for safety or health purposes. Any certification or other statement of compliance with any health or safety-related information in this document shall not be attributable to PMI and is solely the responsibility of the certifier or maker of the statement.

TABLE OF CONTENTS

LIST OF TABLES AND FIGURES

PREFACE

A Guide to the Project Management Body of Knowledge (PMBOK® Guide) – Sixth Edition and other PMI standards provide guidance on the management of portfolios, programs, and projects in order to achieve successful outcomes for those activities. In an organizational environment, portfolios, programs, and projects should be managed in alignment with organizational business strategy and objectives in a manner that will provide the most benefit to the organization.

Organizational project management (OPM) is the framework used to align project, program, and portfolio management practices with organizational strategy and objectives, and customizing or fitting these practices within the organization's context, situation, or structure. This *Standard for Organizational Project Management (OPM)* provides guidance to organizational management, PMO staff, and practitioners on these topics.

This *Standard for Organizational Project Management (OPM)* is a replacement for the previous *Implementing Organizational Project Management: A Practice Guide*, which was published by PMI in 2014, and expands on the content found in that practice guide.

The change in title from *practice guide* to *standard* reflects a change from the procedural-based *how* guidance found in PMI practice guides to a greater emphasis on the principles-based *why* of practicing project management in an organizational setting. Procedural-based guidance of the practice guide has been moved into the appendices of this standard. PMI standards go through a more thorough, rigorous approval process than practice guides, which reflects the maturity of the topic.

This standard is not a replacement for the *Organizational Project Management Maturity Model (OPM3®)* standard, which continues to be published by PMI. The two standards can be used in conjunction with one another. This standard provides guidance to organizations as they implement project management practices at the organizational level and develop capabilities and maturity in that practice. The *OPM3®* standard, as well as other available maturity models, is used as a tool to measure those capabilities, identify areas for improvement, and enhance the level of organizational maturity with regard to the practice of project management.

1

INTRODUCTION

This standard provides guidelines for creating an organizational project management (OPM) framework. OPM entails adapting and aligning practices and processes to provide optimum support for achieving the organization's strategic objectives by means of portfolio, program, and project management. This standard is particularly useful for organizations that do not have a unified project management approach and those in the process of improving or sustaining their current project management framework.

OPM advances organizational capability by developing and linking portfolio, program, and project management principles and practices with organizational enablers and organizational processes to support strategic objectives. Organizational enablers are structural, cultural, technological, or human-resource practices that the performing organization can use to achieve strategic objectives.

1.1 INTENDED AUDIENCE

This standard is intended for practitioners who are involved in portfolio, program, and project management. These practitioners may include but are not limited to:

◆ Executives with responsibility for strategy delivery in for-profit, nonprofit or government divisions, and organizational units;

◆ Executives or managers involved in the support of OPM, such as those responsible for portfolio/program/ project management offices (PMOs) or centers of excellence (COEs);

◆ Any stakeholder involved in the leadership, management, or oversight of portfolios, programs, and/or projects;

◆ Any stakeholder responsible for oversight OPM governance or developing OPM-related policies;

◆ Portfolio, program, and project managers in leadership and liaison positions, such as functional and service delivery managers, who are responsible for OPM-related organizational capabilities;

◆ Process and organizational change professionals (including quality and capability management maturity improvement professionals) who are involved in the design and implementation of portfolio, program, and/or project performance improvement initiatives;

◆ Other management staff who may be responsible for oversight of portfolios, programs, and/or projects;

◆ Members of strategic portfolios, programs, PMOs, and/or COEs; or

◆ Functional managers, including those who manage portfolio, program, and project management professionals.

1.2 OVERVIEW

This standard provides guidelines to assist organizations in identifying, assessing, and applying recognized principles, concepts, methods, and best practices in order to establish and sustain OPM capability. It is intended to enable organizations to better structure the management of their portfolios, programs, and projects in order to achieve strategic objectives. This standard is organized as follows:

◆ **Section 1—Purpose of the Standard for Organizational Project Management.** This section includes an overview of the standard and describes OPM principles, key stakeholders, and essential considerations for implementation. Additionally, this section describes the relevance of OPM and its framework, the intended audience for the standard, and recommendations on how to apply this standard.

◆ **Section 2—Foundational Concepts.** This section describes foundational OPM-essential concepts and factors that contribute to a successful OPM implementation. It discusses what OPM is and how it supports the organization.

◆ **Section 3—Introduction to the OPM Framework.** The OPM framework describes the elements needed to provide ongoing support for OPM as well as the requirements to set up an OPM methodology in any organization. This section provides a description of the framework in terms of core elements including methodology, knowledge management, and talent management to support the implementation of an organizational strategy.

◆ **Section 4—Elements of an OPM Framework within the Organization.** This section describes the identification of an OPM framework, including the tailoring of key OPM elements such as methodology, knowledge management, talent management, and governance.

◆ **Section 5—Implementation of OPM.** This section describes considerations that typically are encountered in an OPM implementation program, such as future operating state design, program organization, business case, and areas of benefits identification. Examples of OPM maturity models are presented to allow understanding of their role in planning and controlling the OPM initiative from a capability identification and development perspective.

◆ **Section 6—Ongoing OPM Management and Monitoring.** This section describes how the organization can ensure that an OPM initiative successfully delivers the planned benefits and that the benefits will be sustained upon completion of the implementation program. It also discusses how long-term monitoring of the implemented OPM system is performed to ensure that it continuously improves the system and realization of benefits.

The appendixes included are as follows:

◆ **Appendix X1.** Contributors and Reviewers of the Standard for Organizational Project Management

◆ **Appendix X2.** Organizational Considerations for OPM Implementation

◆ **Appendix X3.** Recommended Survey Questions Regarding Implementation of OPM Initiatives

◆ **Appendix X4.** How to Develop a Tailored Organizational Project Management Methodology

◆ **Appendix X5.** Organizational Enablers for OPM

1.3 OPM APPROACH

OPM is a framework in which portfolio, program, and project management are integrated with organizational enablers in order to achieve strategic objectives. OPM supports the appropriate balance of knowledge, processes, people, and supportive tools across all functional areas of the organization to provide guidance for its portfolio, program, and project management efforts. Figure 1-1 depicts a systematic OPM approach across all OPM domains that encompasses the following:

◆ **Strategy.** A high-level plan designed to achieve the major goals using internal and external resources from the organization in an effective and efficient manner. Strategic planning is the process of formulating and implementing decisions about an organization's future direction.

◆ **Portfolio value decisions.** Used to effectively select the initiatives in the portfolio that will support the strategy of the organization to achieve the established major long-term objectives.

◆ **Programs and projects.** Used for effective and efficient execution of initiatives aligned with strategies intended to deliver predictable business value.

◆ **Operations.** Operationalizes the initiatives and measures the business value through a benefits realization process.

◆ **Portfolio review and adjustments.** Aligns strategy and organizational resources through a disciplined business value decision process to reflect internal and external changing conditions.

◆ **Business impact analysis.** Analyzes the impact and value from the programs and projects that were implemented and incorporates business results data into the portfolio.

◆ **Value performance analysis.** Provides business value realization data from business value fulfillment back to the strategy of the organization.

◆ **Organizational environment.** Represents the organizational governance, policies, organizational culture and supporting practices of the organization that are created to support OPM and organizational strategy delivery.

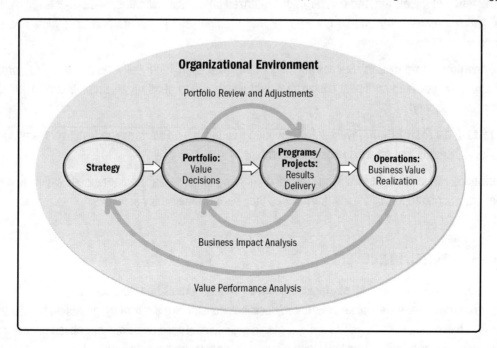

Figure 1-1. Organizational Project Management

Each OPM approach encompasses multiple processes that translate into specific capabilities that an organization should possess in order to improve its maturity and better succeed with its strategy execution. Additionally, the organization needs an environment with demonstrated OPM capabilities to support delivering its strategy and value.

Because OPM describes many capabilities, each organization needs to determine which capabilities are necessary to realize its strategy. For example, a bank in one country may not require the exact same capabilities as a bank in another country or the exact same capabilities as a software development organization.

OPM is based on performing portfolio, program, and project management, coupled with enabling business process and improvement practices conducted in the appropriate manner, to achieve consistent results that align with the strategic priorities. The implementation of business or process improvement practices that support a strategy execution framework does not ensure the achievement of better results. To achieve better results, strategy execution should be combined with the appropriate mix of skilled people using defined processes in order to achieve strategic objectives.

1.3.1 OPM PRINCIPLES

Organizations face challenges as they strive to improve. Organizations need to use resources effectively to efficiently achieve their objectives.

OPM is intended to assist organizations to deliver value and is based on the following principles:

◆ **Alignment with organizational strategy.** All portfolios, programs, and projects should transparently and measurably support organizational strategy.

◆ **Integration with organizational enablers.** Successful alignment, execution, and delivery of portfolios, programs, and projects are predicated on timely cooperation of all directly or indirectly involved practices.

◆ **Consistency of execution and delivery.** All authorized portfolios, programs, and projects should be executed and delivered consistently within governance and methodology parameters in an ethical and professional manner.

◆ **Organizational integration.** Successful alignment, execution, and delivery of portfolios, programs, and projects are predicated on timely cooperation and collaboration of all organization's stakeholders in addition to executive support.

◆ **Value to the organization.** Investing and working within the OPM framework delivers products, services, results, or benefits that outweigh costs to operate it.

◆ **Continuous development.** Tracking and documenting employees' competences, skills, knowledge, and experience acquired formally and informally as they perform their daily activities.

1.3.2 ORGANIZATIONAL STRUCTURE

In many organizations, achieving strategic objectives are accomplished through established processes and governance structures. Executives make investment decisions considering a mix of programs and projects most likely to support the achievement of the organization's strategic objectives. These decisions are based on the organization's risk appetite, resource constraints, and knowledge base (i.e., people, knowledge, and funding).

While executives, managers, and project management practitioners seek improved results through implemented strategies, organizations need to understand the various project-based organizational models that accommodate different situations. Organizational structures, which traditionally may be of many types (e.g., organic, functional, matrix, project-oriented, virtual or hybrid), can affect resource availability and influence how projects are executed. The organizational structure influences the environment in which the project will function within the organization as described in Table 1-1. Various structures should be considered to ensure proper resource allocation and proper approaches and policies to support the delivery of the proposed business plan value. The implementation of OPM requires cross-functional project teams. Team members should be available when the project starts, and in consideration of the organizational structure, the functional manager should support the team members' participation on the project team.

Table 1-1. Influences of Organizational Structures on Projects

Organizational Structure Type	Project Characteristics					
	Work Groups Arranged by:	Project Manager's Authority	Project Manager's Role	Resource Availability	Who Manages the Project Budget?	Project Management Administrative Staff
Organic or Simple	Flexible; people working side-by-side	Little or none	Part-time; may or may not be a designated job role like coordinator	Little or none	Owner or operator	Little or none
Functional (centralized)	Job being done (e.g., engineering, manufacturing)	Little or none	Part-time; may or may not be a designated job role like coordinator	Little or none	Functional manager	Part-time
Multidivisional (may replicate functions for each division with little centralization)	One of: product; production processes; portfolio; program; geographic region; customer type	Little or none	Part-time; may or may not be a designated job role like coordinator	Little or none	Functional manager	Part-time
Matrix – strong	By job function, with project manager as a function	Moderate to high	Full-time designated job role	Moderate to high	Project manager	Full-time
Matrix – weak	Job function	Low	Part-time; done as part of another job and not a designated job role like coordinator	Low	Functional manager	Part-time
Matrix – balanced	Job function	Low to moderate	Part-time; embedded in the functions as a skill and may not be a designated job role like coordinator	Low to moderate	Mixed	Part-time
Project-oriented (composite, hybrid)	Project	High to almost total	Full-time designated job role	High to almost total	Project manager	Full-time
Virtual	Network structure with nodes at points of contact with other people	Low to moderate	Full-time or part-time	Low to moderate	Mixed	Could be full-time or part-time
Hybrid	Mix of other types	Mixed	Mixed	Mixed	Mixed	Mixed
PMO*	Mix of other types	High to almost total	Full-time designated job role	High to almost total	Project manager	Full-time

*PMO refers to a portfolio, program, or project management office or organization.

Portfolio, program, and project management requires deliberate planning and action to create the optimal conditions for success. This entails implementing strategy, leadership, goals, processes, skills, systems, issue resolution, complexity navigation, risk mitigation, and structure to direct and exploit the dynamic nature of project execution. However, when strategy moves from the boardroom to operations, the ability to consistently and successfully deliver by using project management is sometimes overlooked.

Regardless of the organization type—organic, functional, multidivisional, matrix, or project-oriented, virtual or hybrid—the strategic alignment should have a cross-functional dynamic. Members of all functional areas should comply with the program and project teams to meet the end objective.

Assuming the organization is not project oriented, the customary way of working will change:

◆ Employees will work on projects as a temporary assignment but still report to a functional area.

◆ A new generation of project managers will evolve from business functions.

◆ Many other changes will be experienced.

These changes require organizations to adopt an integrated project approach including structures such as a governance-oriented enterprise project management office (EPMO) (see Sections 1.6.2 and 1.6.3 for more information). These structures should enable organizations to promote the implementation of OPM. When adopted, an EPMO aims to ensure strategic alignment of the portfolio initiatives to the strategic objectives. The EPMO provides governance, structure, process, and procedures to control operations and changes to performance objectives and benefits management.

An integrated leadership, management, and supportive environment is critical for the management of portfolios, programs, and projects, as are other operational and support functions, such as technical support or customer service. The EPMO should tightly integrate its planning, execution, and monitoring processes with the management of the operational part of the organization. This will help to ensure the appropriate balance between program and project activities and business operations, including optimal use of the organization's resources.

Successful organizations achieve strategic objectives when:

◆ Portfolio, program, and project management practices are aligned to the strategy;

◆ The organization provides executives with visibility and uses active executive sponsors on projects; and

◆ The organization uses methods to manage change effectively, hires qualified project managers, and delivers projects that achieve strategic objectives.

1.3.3 OPM FRAMEWORK

The OPM framework supports balance and coordination between project and business management in support of organizational strategy (see Figure 1-2). The OPM framework needs to be visibly supported and properly communicated across the organization to become a priority to both management and practitioners involved in the implementation of OPM.

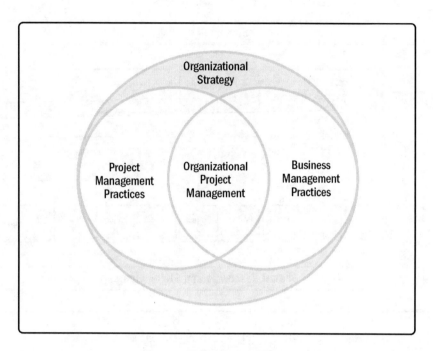

Figure 1-2. OPM Framework

The OPM framework provides the basis for the implementation of OPM to help the organization align resources to achieve its strategic objectives. It is important to understand the relationships among portfolios, programs, and projects in order to understand OPM. A portfolio refers to a collection of projects, programs, subsidiary portfolios, and operations managed as a group to achieve strategic objectives. Programs include related projects, subsidiary programs, and program activities managed in a coordinated manner to obtain benefits not available from managing them individually. Individual projects that are either within or outside of a program are still considered part of a portfolio. Although the projects or programs within a portfolio may not necessarily be interdependent or directly related, they are linked to the organization's strategic plan by means of the organization's portfolio plan.

Figure 1-3 shows how the portfolio is linked to organizational strategy and the relationships among portfolios, programs, and projects, as well as between programs and individual projects.

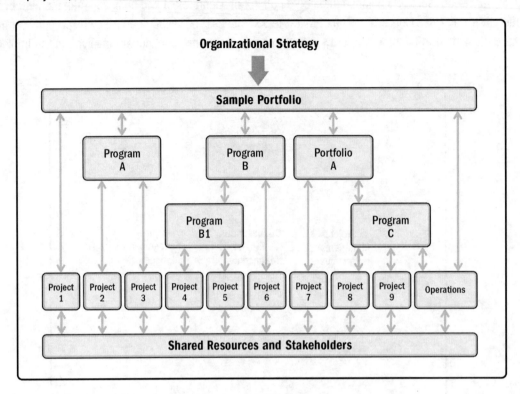

Figure 1-3. Portfolio, Program, and Project Management Interactions

OPM as part of organizational planning includes the prioritization and selection of programs and projects based on components relevant to the organization's strategic plan. Criteria such as resources availability, risk factors, line of business, expected benefits, types of projects, funding, market analysis, and direction of short- and long-term vision are crucial in the alignment of the portfolio and determine the future success of programs and projects.

The need for OPM emerged from increased project management knowledge and practices. The emergence of the PMO and EPMO and use of best practices and standards has enhanced the understanding of the management of programs and portfolios. The OPM framework provides flexibility to accommodate methodologies and approaches. In traditional project management, the nature of portfolios, programs, and projects is not the same; therefore, a single methodology may not be the best solution. It is important to establish a set of approaches from which the best choice for a particular portfolio, program, or project can be selected.

The use of different approaches (methodologies) for executing portfolios, programs, and projects is often desirable within the organization's OPM framework so that the expected strategic results and benefits are delivered or achieved. The OPM methodology should:

◆ Encourage selection of methods and provide guidance on choosing the appropriate approach.

◆ Adapt to changes in the OPM framework driven by internal and external threats, acquisition of new capabilities, new government regulations, and geopolitical changes in the marketplace, among others.

The OPM framework is supported by processes such as governance, change management, and process management; it helps to define the portfolio and how it needs to evolve in order to keep strategic alignment. The OPM methodology defines the execution approach of the portfolio. The OPM framework enables the organization to manage and monitor progress so that programs and projects produce the expected benefits.

1.3.4 ORGANIZATIONAL BENEFITS OF OPM

OPM promotes the effective integration of business objectives and practices along with portfolio, program, and project management to effectively implement strategy that generates business value. Other potential benefits are possible, as shown in Figure 1-4.

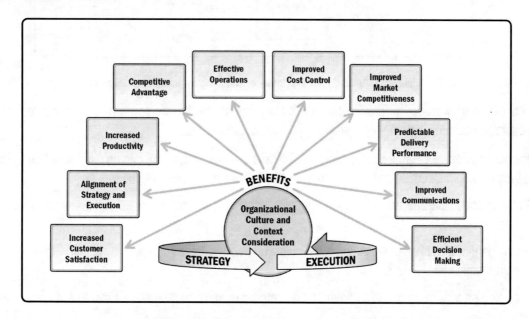

Figure 1-4. Potential OPM Benefits for Organizations

Benefits often build incrementally. Executives should consider and plan the selection, progression, and realization of expected benefits by investing in OPM practices in order to deliver better business outcomes and sustainable long-term business value. During times of economic downturn, this investment becomes even more important, because adherence to project management methods and strategies reduces risks, cuts costs, and improves success rates, which are vital to surviving during an economic crisis.

The OPM integrator and the organizational change team will be integrating and orchestrating operations in a manner that both realizes and sustains benefits (see Section 5.3.5).

1.4 HOW TO USE THIS STANDARD

Figure 1-5 reflects the high-level inputs to and outcomes from using this standard. This standard is intended to assist executives with developing or improving an OPM framework that integrates the organization's business model, enterprise environmental factors (EEF), organizational process assets (OPA), and generally accepted portfolio, program, and project management standards.

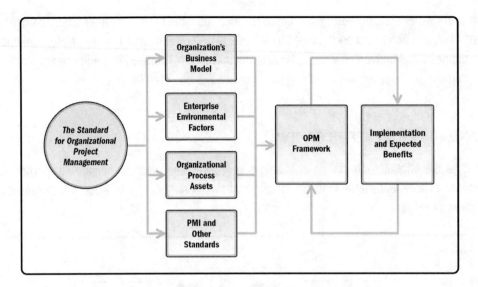

Figure 1-5. General Flow and Intended Outcomes of Using This Standard

PMI standards are intended to provide information and instruction for the application of standards and/or best practices for project management. Key purposes of this standard include:

◆ Providing guidelines that are consistent with OPM maturity models, which can be used to determine capability gaps between the current state of the organization and the desired future state;

◆ Defining capabilities as the collection of people, processes, and technologies that enable an organization to deliver OPM;

◆ Providing direction to an organization to develop a knowledge-based competency in line with market or sector requirements; and

◆ Providing an organization with a minimum competency required to effectively move in a strategic direction.

1.5 RELATIONSHIPS AMONG PORTFOLIO, PROGRAM, AND PROJECT MANAGEMENT AND OPM

In order to understand their relationship with OPM, it is important to understand portfolio, program, and project management, the similarities and differences among these disciplines, and their relationship with OPM.

Portfolio, program, and project management are aligned with or driven by organizational strategy. However portfolio, program, project management interact at different levels to achieve strategic goals and objectives:

◆ **Portfolio management.** Portfolio management aligns with organizational strategies by selecting the appropriate programs or projects, prioritizing the work, and providing the needed resources.

◆ **Program management.** Program management harmonizes its program and project components, controls interdependencies, and manages transformational change in order to realize specified benefits.

◆ **Project management.** Project management develops and implements plans to achieve a specific scope that is driven by the objectives of the portfolio or program to which it is subjected and ultimately to organizational strategies.

◆ **OPM.** OPM advances organizational capability by linking portfolio, program, and project management principles and practices with organizational enablers (e.g., structural, cultural, technological, and human resource practices) to support strategic objectives. An organization measures its capabilities, then plans and implements improvements toward the systematic achievement of best practices appropriate for its appetite for change and its desired future state.

For definitions of these terms, refer to the Glossary at the end of this standard.

Table 1-2 shows the comparison of portfolio, program, and project views across several aspects within an organization.

An organization that implements OPM can improve its processes by adopting recognized practices to achieve consistent portfolio, program, and project success in support of strategic objectives.

Table 1-2. Comparative Overview of Portfolio, Program, and Project Management

Organizational Project Management			
	Projects	**Programs**	**Portfolios**
Definition	A project is a temporary endeavor undertaken to create a unique product, service, or result.	A program is a group of related projects, subsidiary programs, and program activities that are managed in a coordinated manner to obtain benefits not available from managing them individually.	A portfolio is a collection of projects, programs, subsidiary portfolios, and operations managed as a group to achieve strategic objectives.
Scope	Projects have defined objectives. Scope is progressively elaborated throughout the project life cycle.	Programs have a scope that encompasses the scopes of its program components. Programs produce benefits to an organization by ensuring that the outputs and outcomes of program components are delivered in a coordinated and complementary manner.	Portfolios have an organizational scope that changes with the strategic objectives of the organization.
Change	Project managers expect change and implement processes to keep change managed and controlled.	Programs are managed in a manner that accepts and adapts to change as necessary to optimize the delivery of benefits as the program's components deliver outcomes and/or outputs.	Portfolio managers continuously monitor changes in the broader internal and external environments.
Planning	Project managers progressively elaborate high-level information into detailed plans throughout the project life cycle.	Programs are managed using high-level plans that track the interdependencies and progress of program components. Program plans are also used to guide planning at the component level.	Portfolio managers create and maintain necessary processes and communication relative to the aggregate portfolio.
Management	Project managers manage the project team to meet the project objectives.	Programs are managed by program managers who ensure that program benefits are delivered as expected, by coordinating the activities of a program's components.	Portfolio managers may manage or coordinate portfolio management staff, or program and project staff that may have reporting responsibilities into the aggregate portfolio.
Monitoring	Project managers monitor and control the work of producing the products, services, or results that the project was undertaken to produce.	Program managers monitor the progress of program components to ensure the overall goals, schedules, budget, and benefits of the program will be met.	Portfolio managers monitor strategic changes and aggregate resource allocation, performance results, and risk of the portfolio.
Success	Success is measured by product and project quality, timeliness, budget compliance, and degree of customer satisfaction.	A program's success is measured by the program's ability to deliver its intended benefits to an organization, and by the program's efficiency and effectiveness in delivering those benefits.	Success is measured in terms of the aggregate investment performance and benefit realization of the portfolio.

1.6 ORGANIZATIONAL STRATEGY

OPM bridges the gap between the organization's vision and mission with portfolio, program, and projects underway, through coordination, alignment, and implementation to meet the organization's strategic objectives.

Understanding the organizational strategy is one of the initial steps that serves as the foundation during an OPM implementation. Gaining knowledge of the organization's strategy provides the basis for understanding where the organization wants to go and how it wants to get there.

A common organizational goal is to achieve the expected strategic objectives and benefits consistently. The challenge of aligning business units' operations with larger mission objectives for the entire organization is the driving force behind the implementation of project management framework, processes, and practices.

OPM allows the incorporation of project management practices with business and operation's processes as a business unit function inside the organizational structure.

Meeting strategic objectives by consistently completing initiatives that produce the desired benefits is a goal of many organizations. Many organizations find it difficult to keep their business units aligned with corporate/business initiatives and objectives and with the organization's philosophy and mission. This is one of the driving forces influencing organizations to implement and align project management practices and processes on an organization-wide basis. The challenge is how to incorporate project management into business operations, and how to integrate project management as a business function and culture into the organizational structure.

Projects are an integral part of business, because they contribute to benefits that enable the achievement of strategic objectives as well as enhance customer and stakeholder satisfaction. Strategic alignment helps organizations to properly implement project management principles, processes, and practices. This can have a significant impact on an organization's time to market, cost to market, quality to market, and customers' recognition of the organization as a world-class leader.

Executives and business unit heads need to recognize that managing strategically aligned projects has a significant impact on achieving organizational strategy. Their ability to successfully manage projects depends on the proper application of specific project management processes, knowledge, skills, tools, and techniques. Therefore, it makes sense to establish ownership and management of project management practices at an organization-wide level.

1.6.1 OPM MATURITY MODELS

OPM maturity models are often cited as tools for measuring an organization's adoption and consistent implementation of recommended practices in project management that help to achieve strategic objectives. A recommended practice is an activity that is considered effective, delivers value to the organization that implements it, and is beneficial for OPM maturity. The common sources for recommended practices are global standards and organizational lessons learned.

Adopting recommended practices is only the first step in process maturity. Without ensuring the continuous improvement of these processes, further development of these processes could result in processes that do not fit their application, are not consistently followed, or do not deliver value as expected. For further discussion on maturity models, see Section 5.5.

1.6.2 PMO AND OPM

Program and project management offices are management structures that standardize the program and project-related governance processes and facilitate the sharing of resources, methodologies, tools, and techniques. A PMO is an organizational body assigned with various responsibilities related to the centralized and coordinated management of the programs and projects under its authority. During an OPM implementation, the PMO ensures the proper strategic alignment of portfolios, programs, and projects and reflects the results in corporate measurement systems such as the balanced scorecard.

A PMO may be delegated with the authority to act as an executive stakeholder and a key decision maker to make recommendations to terminate projects because of changes in the organizational strategy, or to take other actions, as required, to keep programs and projects aligned with business objectives. Additionally, the PMO may be involved in the selection, management, and deployment of shared or dedicated project resources. The primary functions of a PMO may include, but are not limited to:

◆ Reporting directly to executives, independent of other organizational functional groups;

◆ Integrating the application of project management practices with operational business practices by coaching, mentoring, training, and oversight;

◆ Coordinating portfolio management activities and ensuring alignment between organizational strategy and programs and projects;

◆ Coordinating communication across programs and projects;

◆ Developing and managing project policies, procedures, templates, and other project documentation (organizational process assets);

◆ Identifying and developing project management methodology, recommended practices, and standards;

◆ Managing shared resources across all projects administered by the PMO;

◆ Monitoring compliance with project management standards, policies, procedures, and templates by means of project audits;

◆ Engaging the portfolio, program, and project management community and ensuring their involvement in continuous improvement of the OPM framework; and

◆ Providing centralized support for managing changes and tracking risks and issues.

1.6.3 ENTERPRISE PROJECT MANAGEMENT OFFICE (EPMO)

The enterprise/organization PMO (EPMO) is the highest-level PMO in an organization This PMO is often responsible for (a) aligning program and project work with organizational strategy, (b) establishing and ensuring appropriate enterprise governance, and (c) performing portfolio management functions to ensure strategy alignment and benefits realization. The EPMO may apply governance at the enterprise level and may incorporate strategy development and strategic planning support. The EPMO may have direct responsibility for, or influence over, other lower-level PMOs. The EPMO may also be responsible for supporting data management, coordination of governance and reporting, and administrative activities to support the project or program team. Management of multiple stakeholders and ensuring continuous communication are additional, important roles of the EPMO.

1.7 OPM STAKEHOLDERS

A major success factor in projects is the identification and engagement of stakeholders from the start. Stakeholders are individuals, groups, or organizations that may affect, be affected by, or perceive themselves to be affected by a decision, activity, or outcome of a portfolio, program, or project. Many stakeholders provide valuable input and play a critical role in the success of any program or project. They may also be inclined to positively or adversely impact the achievement of project objectives based on the benefits or threats they perceive. Therefore, it is essential that key stakeholders be identified by including their positions, level of influence, financial support, and source of power. Stakeholders may be internal or external to the organization. Within an organization, internal stakeholders can belong to any level of the organization's hierarchy.

Key stakeholders of an OPM initiative include, but are not limited to, the following:

◆ **Executives.** The organization's executives that share the strategy with PMO and project management teams to align the overall business strategy at a portfolio level to implement OPM successfully.

◆ **OPM governance board.** The group responsible for ensuring that OPM goals are achieved, for steering the OPM organization, for making important decisions, and for providing support in addressing risks and issues.

◆ **OPM sponsor.** A person or group that provides resources and support for the OPM initiative and is accountable for its overall success.

◆ **OPM customer.** An individual or organization that promotes the use of new OPM capabilities and supports the investment in capability delivery, for example, program and project sponsors or business unit managers.

◆ **OPM practitioners.** Individuals who are subject matter experts in OPM assessment and implementation. They work with organizations to assess project management competency and to develop an implementation plan focusing on the practices that the organization should apply based on priorities, attainability, benefits, and cost.

◆ **Performing organization.** The group that is performing the work.

◆ **PMO/EPMO.** An organizational body assigned various responsibilities related to the strategic alignment, centralization, and coordination of portfolios, programs, and projects.

◆ **Portfolio/program/project managers.** Individuals responsible for managing portfolios, programs, and projects. They are responsible for driving the transition to the new future state and its operational adoption in order to achieve the expected organizational benefits associated with the strategic objectives.

◆ **Supplier.** An individual or organization that provides goods and services to the organization.

◆ **Beneficiary.** An individual or organization that benefits from the use of the new capabilities.

◆ **Regulatory and statutory authorities.** Norms and laws of local, national, or regional authorities that affect the project.

◆ **Competitor.** An organization that could take commercial or economic business away from the organization.

◆ **Potential customer.** An individual or organization that is liable to become a purchaser of products and/or services from an organization.

2

FOUNDATIONAL CONCEPTS

2.1 INTRODUCTION

This section builds the case for organizational project management (OPM) initiatives and is a resource for OPM leaders and executives. It describes the concepts of OPM and what is needed for a successful OPM initiative.

2.2 INVESTING IN OPM AND ADDING VALUE

Organizations often invest in aspects of project management based on significant issues in the organization. These significant issues lead to conversations about project management and small tactical investments to avert the next significant issue or to show improvements from the last significant issue. These tactical investments include items such as:

◆ Temporary addition of resources,

◆ Project management training, and

◆ Tool implementation.

Although each of these tactical solutions provides some level of improvement and may generate some short-term incremental improvements, most of the time these solutions do not address the real issues that an organization is facing. Organizations in crisis may face loss of market share, sale or acquisition, and governmental threats or sanctions. These tactical remedies support individual project success versus project success in delivering the organizational strategy. An organization that invests in OPM can preempt and address the real issues directly to support the organization and not only the projects. OPM builds a dynamic organization that deals with change effectively, a project is essentially a change in management.

Investment in organizational project management requires careful consideration of the organization's strategic objectives and business drivers:

◆ Organizations seeking an operational efficiency strategy should gain control of project budget and value generated.

◆ Organizations that follow a customer intimacy strategy should improve the alignment between the marketing and delivery teams.

◆ Organizations that follow a product innovation strategy should be concerned with time to market, innovation, creativity, and human resources.

◆ Organizations that seek economic growth should tie significantly to value realizations that include growth, increased reputation, market share, and customer retention.

OPM changes the investment approach from a reactive to a proactive one targeted at value creation for the organization. The change management process for such an undertaking can be significant. However, organizations that shift to this investment approach realize the benefits of proactive alignment with strategy and better strategic execution than organizations that use tactical or crisis-driven investment approaches.

2.3 BUSINESS VALUE

PMI defines business value as the net quantifiable benefit derived from a business endeavor. The benefit may be tangible, intangible, or both. Organizations create value by effective utilization of their business models after business analysis. Some organizations deliver value through operations while others use projects for this purpose. Through the effective use of portfolio, program, and project management, organizations have the capability to increase their potential to create value and, in some cases, directly increase the effectiveness and efficiency of the value creation itself. This is achieved by employing reliable, established OPM processes to meet strategic objectives and to use the full potential of the assumed business model. Whether an organization is a government agency or a nonprofit or for-profit organization, all organizations focus on attaining business value from their activities.

Business value realization begins with comprehensive strategic planning and management. Organizational strategy is expressed through the organization's vision and mission, including orientation to markets, competition, and other environmental factors. Effective organizational strategy provides defined directions for development and growth, in addition to performance metrics for success. Portfolio, program, and project management techniques are essential for addressing the gap between organizational strategy and business value realization.

Organizations can further facilitate the alignment of these portfolio, program, and project management activities by strengthening organizational enablers such as structural, cultural, technological, and human resource practices. Organizations can achieve successful transitions by continuously conducting portfolio strategic alignment and optimization, performing business impact analyses, and developing robust organizational enablers.

2.4 OPM BUSINESS CASE

A business case is an essential component for establishing an OPM framework. In order to gain support for OPM implementation, chief executive officers (CEOs) and their leadership teams, along with key stakeholders, need the details to explain why an OPM framework is needed and what business problems it will prevent or solve. In addition, the business case should include a description of the characteristics of an OPM framework in which there can be many variations (see Section 5 for more information). Once the needs and challenges of the business are understood, the OPM characteristics can be defined. To support the definition, additional facts and data help emphasize why OPM is needed to deliver organizational strategy. This analysis should also verify the current mutual impact of programs, projects, and other business operations within the organization.

Like any change to an organization, an understanding of the current state is essential to support the business case. Executives should seek to understand how programs and projects are delivered currently and the associated issues or gaps that may be addressed through OPM. This strengthens the case for change and how OPM can improve portfolio, program, and project delivery and benefits to meet the strategic goals of the organization.

The remaining component of a business case for OPM is a definition of key performance indicators (KPIs). Typical KPIs include measures and metrics comparing current state to the future state, quality of the work completed, and overall management of the project including sponsor engagement.

2.4.1 OPM SPONSORSHIP

Clearly stated expectations are key to ensuring the establishment of sponsorship and defined expectations and behavior needed by the organization's executives. Sponsorship is required for a successful OPM implementation. The most effective organizations recognize the need for portfolio, program, and project management in everything that they do related to the successful execution of the organizational strategy. This is why these organizations also establish OPM with proper management authority, support, resources, and tools within the operational structure of the business. It is vital that executives understand OPM and its direct impact on their own capability to deliver the organization's strategic objectives. Executives should clearly communicate their buy-in for OPM throughout the organization and support it actively.

To create a culture that embraces project management and to increase the business value OPM brings to the organization, OPM needs a complete framework with clear direction, governance, and support. The portfolio, program, or project teams should be adequately funded, staffed with skilled personnel, and have access to executives. These expectations for sponsorship need to be part of the business case and specifically, the key decisions requested of executives need to be part of the business case.

2.4.2 THE VALUE PROPOSITION

The act of establishing OPM does not by itself increase the effectiveness of implementing an organizational strategy. The crucial factor is how OPM is executed and sustained, and which areas are prioritized for improvement. This determines how successful an organization is at delivering programs and projects. OPM has a greater impact and is most effective when the benefits realized for the programs and supporting projects are documented with measures in place. This includes activities such as planning change, measuring its benefits, and planning that results in improved delivery. It is essential that the organization and sponsoring body have clear business objectives for implementing OPM (or enhancing its role, if already in place) in terms of costs and performance improvement.

2.4.3 BENEFITS SUSTAINMENT

The purpose of benefits sustainment is to ensure that the initial benefits have been transitioned to the appropriate entities or subsequent programs to lead the ongoing post-transition work. When the initial OPM program is closed, responsibility for sustaining the benefits provided by the program may pass to another organization. Benefits are sustained through operations, maintenance, new projects and/or programs, or other efforts. A benefits sustainment plan should be developed and management established prior to program closure to identify the risks, processes, measures, metrics, and tools necessary to ensure the continued realization of the benefits delivered.

The sponsor, program manager, and other stakeholders should plan ongoing sustainment of program benefits during the performance of the initial program. The actual work to ensure the sustainment of benefits is typically conducted after the close of the initial program and is beyond the scope of the individual component projects. Although a recipient (person, organization, or beneficiary group) performs work after the program ends, the program manager is responsible for planning post-transition activities during program execution.

A PMO or similar organization is a typical key success factor in OPM implementation benefits sustainment. This structure ties into the governance of OPM and the organization.

2.4.4 ELEMENTS OF THE OPM BUSINESS CASE

Facts and data (inclusive of historical events and future trends forecasts) are key elements of the business case. Both internal and external data are used to support the business case for an OPM implementation.

Internal success stories are helpful in creating the business case for an OPM implementation. These stories stress the importance that portfolio, program, and project management play in an organization's successful execution of its strategy.

Analysis of lessons learned inefficiencies and/or past failures can also be constructively used to build the business case for OPM. It is essential that lessons from inefficiencies and/or past failures are turned into concrete arguments. Examples could include (a) costs of doubled resources in projects (e.g., software licenses, underutilized equipment or experts), (b) repeated mistakes or disturbances in critical operations, (c) penalties or warranty costs caused by poor project execution, and (d) consultancy in the areas where organization already has established experience. Reduction of these negative situations often provide clear return on investment in OPM.

In the business case, it is important to emphasize that results in one area of the business are transferable to others. The business case should also highlight how well recently completed programs and projects support the organizational strategy. In sharing these findings in the business case, other executives will want to obtain these results in their lines of business. This is a key part of why an OPM implementation is essential to the organization.

In addition, there are also external data points available in support of building the business case for OPM. PMI and other organizations have data that show the ROI (return on investment) for standardized methodology, practices, processes, and benefits realized. Leveraging external data also strengthens the case for establishing OPM.

2.4.5 ESTABLISHING A BASELINE FOR THE BUSINESS CASE

Establishing a baseline of the current project management maturity as part of the business case helps executives visualize the state of maturity of the organization. A baseline assessment allows each area in the organization to understand the current state of its project management maturity in order to build a plan to address the gaps in processes, tools, and behavior. Appendix X3 contains a simple assessment, which is valuable in understanding any repeatable project management practices within the organization.

3

INTRODUCTION TO THE OPM FRAMEWORK

3.1 INTRODUCTION

The organizational project management (OPM) framework describes the elements that are required to provide ongoing support. This section provides a description of the framework in terms of the core elements of methodology, knowledge management, and talent management. To enhance OPM to support the realization of an organization's strategy, a relevant governance framework is also critical for success. The critical elements of the OPM framework (Figure 3-1), are as follows:

- ◆ **OPM methodology.** The system of practices, techniques, procedures, and rules used in OPM.

- ◆ **Knowledge management.** The creation, sharing, and use of experience, values and beliefs, contextual information, intuition, and insights to address the needs of the organization.

- ◆ **Talent management.** An organization's approach to retaining and developing its people with regard to knowledge, performance, and personal competence in order to increase the likelihood of delivering outcomes that meet stakeholders' requirements.

- ◆ **OPM governance.** The framework, functions, and processes for OPM activities in order to align portfolio, program, and project management practices to meet organizational and strategic goals. For additional information, refer to *Governance of Portfolios, Programs, and Projects: A Practice Guide* [1].[1]

More detailed information on each of the topics covered can be found in Section 4.

Figure 3-1 depicts the critical elements of an OPM framework such as OPM methodology, knowledge management, and talent management where OPM governance ensures the alignment of the other three elements to the organizational strategy. OPM methodology falls within the jurisdiction of OPM governance; however in many cases, aspects of talent and knowledge management may not completely fall within the jurisdiction of OPM governance.

---

[1] The numbers in brackets refer to the list of references at the end of this standard.

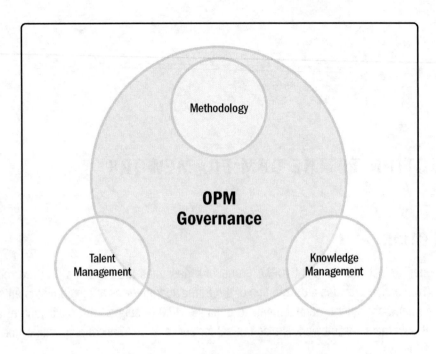

Figure 3-1. Critical Elements of OPM Framework

3.2 OPM METHODOLOGIES

This section introduces OPM methodologies by building on the descriptions of methodologies and project management methodologies as follows:

◆ **Methodology.** A system of practices, techniques, procedures, and rules used by those who work in a discipline.

◆ **Project management methodologies.** Methodologies intended for those who work in the discipline of project management. Project management methodologies aim to provide advice, directions, and instructions on portfolio, program, and project management.

◆ **OPM methodologies.** Project management methodologies intended for those who work in project management within a specific organization. OPM methodologies aim to provide advice, directions, knowledge, and instructions on portfolio, program, and/or project management relevant to specific organizational backgrounds, circumstances, motives, and needs.

More detailed information on OPM methodologies can be found in Section 4.2.

3.3 KNOWLEDGE MANAGEMENT

Knowledge management is a concept involving an organization's deliberate, focused, and efficient handling of the organization's knowledge assets to generate, collect, organize, and analyze its knowledge in terms of documentation, storage, resources, and people skills/competences. Knowledge management should support the OPM model defined for the organization to drive consistency of execution and delivery in line with the OPM principles defined in Section 1.3.1. In addition, more detailed information is available in Section 4.3.

Organizations may already have resources dedicated to internal knowledge management efforts. These resources are often part of their organizational strategy and resource management systems.

Knowledge management efforts typically focus on organizational objectives such as improved performance, innovation, sharing lessons learned, integration, and organizational continuous improvement. These efforts may overlap with organizational learning, whereas knowledge management has a greater focus on the management of knowledge as a strategic asset with a focus on encouraging knowledge sharing, which includes tacit knowledge. The main objective of knowledge management is to enable organizational learning. Organizational learning is the way new knowledge is created, retained, and transferred, which is purely based on applying knowledge for a purpose and learning from the process and the outcome.

The outcomes to knowledge management are:

◆ Understanding how to create the best-in-class organizational learning environment,

◆ Awareness of how and why something has been learned,

◆ Experienced-based learning,

◆ Assurance that the learning that takes place is useful to the organization, and

◆ System for making the critical knowledge available to the right person at the right time in the appropriate manner.

In order to obtain benefits from these outcomes, knowledge management should cover a complete knowledge life cycle, up to the moment when knowledge is successfully applied and used to benefit actual initiatives within the organization. More detailed information on the knowledge management life cycle can be found in Section 4.3.

3.4 TALENT MANAGEMENT

For any organization adopting an OPM framework, it is essential to have an effective talent management process and supporting framework. PMI states, "At the heart of successful strategy execution is the ability to attract, retain, and make the best use of project management talent" [2]. This is aligned and in accordance with the OPM principles defined in Section 1.3.1 and, in particular, consistency of execution and delivery, which is reliant upon effective talent management.

Talent management and development is more than ensuring that the individuals have the necessary knowledge. Effective portfolio, program, and project managers consistently apply knowledge and personal behaviors to increase the likelihood of delivering portfolios, programs, and projects that meet stakeholders' requirements.

Competence refers to the demonstrated ability to perform activities within a portfolio, program, or project environment that leads to expected outcomes based on defined and accepted standards. It is important to align talent management and project management to support the model defined for the organization to best deliver.

Portfolio, program, and project manager competence consists of three separate aspects:

◆ **Knowledge competence.** What the portfolio, program, or project manager knows about the application of processes, tools, and techniques for portfolio, program, or project activities.

◆ **Performance competence.** How the portfolio, program, or project manager applies portfolio, program, or project management knowledge to meet stakeholder requirements.

◆ **Personal competence.** How portfolio, program, or project managers behave when performing activities within the portfolio, program, or project environment. This includes their ethics, professional conduct, attitude, and core personality characteristics, and how these are demonstrated in their leadership style.

An organization needs to ensure that its portfolio, program, and project management capabilities are optimized for the types of programs and projects that it undertakes. This may result in additional competences that are specific to the organization or industry. These can be considered as supplementary to personal competences. Staff should know how they can progress their career within the organization as they move on to different portfolios, programs, and projects.

Some of the key benefits to the organization for implementing a competency framework include but are not limited to:

◆ Motivated portfolio, program, and project management community;

◆ Individuals who have an understanding of their professional development needs;

◆ Portfolio, program, and project managers who are better positioned to provide maximum value to the organization and serve the needs of the business;

◆ Organizations that are better positioned not only to attract the best talent, but also to retain the talent;

◆ Individuals who are assigned to and aligned with the most appropriate opportunities commensurate with their competences and development needs; and

◆ Ability to reward the right people appropriately through measurable competences linked to personal/ organizational performance.

Reference should also be made to The PMI Talent Triangle® and *PMI's Pulse of the Profession In-Depth Report: Talent Management*, which states that success is reinforced by not only project technical management, but also leadership, along with strategic and business management skills [3]. Developing competences in these areas is a significant factor in how a project manager performs.

More detailed information on talent management can be found in Section 4.4.

3.5 OPM GOVERNANCE

OPM governance is the framework, functions, and guidance in order to align portfolio, program, and project management practices to meet organizational strategic and operational goals. OPM governance should be developed vertically, throughout the organizational chart, and horizontally, throughout projects, to create integrity and harmony across the business and projects. Additional information is available in Section 4.5.

Organizational governance encompasses the entire organization, focusing on setting the strategic direction, legal, fiduciary, and oversight functions along with boundaries. OPM governance is a subset of organizational governance and includes the policies, procedures, and systems through which executives direct, define, authorize, and support the alignment of portfolios, programs, and projects with strategy and organizational goals. The governance approach should be designed to make managing the project-based initiatives as efficient and effective as possible. As an overriding responsibility, organizations should be structured and tasked with making projects successful. This reflects the OPM principle of organizational strategy alignment described in Section 1.3.1.

OPM governance complies with the OPM principle for consistency of planning, design, execution, and delivery by ensuring that portfolios, programs, and projects are conceived and executed according to the methodologies and standards established by the organization.

OPM fosters a tailored approach to governance that takes into account the politics, culture, external stakeholders, environment, and regulatory factors in organizations. Different levels of governance may be required based on these influences and factors. It is also important to create visibility as to how OPM governance is being applied across the organization and by whom. More detailed information on OPM governance can be found in Section 4.5.

4

ELEMENTS OF AN OPM FRAMEWORK WITHIN THE ORGANIZATION

4.1 INTRODUCTION

This section describes the organizational project management (OPM) framework, including the tailoring of OPM elements such as methodology, knowledge management, talent management, and governance.

4.2 OPM METHODOLOGIES

Referring to Section 3.2, OPM methodologies are project management methodologies intended for those who work in project management within a specific organization. OPM methodologies aim to provide advice, directions, knowledge, and instructions on portfolio, program, and/or project management relevant to specific organizational backgrounds, circumstances, motives, and needs.

OPM methodologies may be further characterized as groups of interrelated project management processes and practices. OPM methodologies seek to increase the probability of project success and to enhance project effectiveness and efficiency. Organizations implement and use OPM methodologies in a coordinated way to obtain outcomes, benefits, and control not available from employing tools, techniques, and methods individually.

OPM methodologies are established, operated (i.e., tailored and applied), maintained, and enhanced by organizations from all sectors, business areas, locations, and cultures in order to gain benefits for the organization, its projects, and its customers. OPM methodologies are typically used for reasons such as:

◆ Establishing a common way of working on projects,

◆ Providing structure to projects,

◆ Standardizing projects and providing consistency,

◆ Providing common project language and vocabulary,

◆ Enhancing the quality of project management,

◆ Circulating best practices and lessons learned (i.e., avoiding "reinventing the wheel"),

◆ Defining roles and responsibilities,

◆ Facilitating effective collaboration between teams and departments, and

◆ Enhancing OPM in general.

Organizations may employ OPM methodologies for reasons pertaining to sector, industry, business areas, and/or the organization itself, including but not limited to:

◆ Evaluation and comparison of project issues,

◆ Exchanging and sharing of project staff, and

◆ Maintaining reputation and supporting sales and marketing.

Please see Sections 1.3.4 and 5.4 for information on typical OPM benefits.

Organizations develop and improve OPM methodologies by establishing and combining those portfolio, program, and/or project methodology elements considered most likely to provide the expected benefits. OPM methodologies are more complicated than simple collections of methodology elements. OPM methodologies realize their full potential when elements are coordinated and interrelated. Some of the elements that organizations use in OPM methodologies are:

◆ Cost management;

◆ Schedule management;

◆ Risk (threat and opportunity) management;

◆ Information management, including communicating and reporting;

◆ Project staff onboarding and training;

◆ Selectable methodology elements (light/standard/comprehensive approach);

◆ Stakeholder management;

◆ Portfolio, program, and project life cycle management;

◆ Scope management;

◆ Issue management;

◆ Quality management;

◆ Requirement management;

◆ Procurement management;

◆ Resource management;

◆ Configuration management;

◆ Benefits management; and

◆ Change management.

Organizations may also employ elements specific to the industry sector, business area, and/or organization, including:

◆ Alternative portfolio, program, and project life cycles;

◆ Organizational business processes or connections; and

◆ Organizational product processes or connections.

OPM methodologies are more complicated than simple collections of project management tools, techniques, and methods. OPM methodologies provide their full potential only when the contents are coordinated and interrelated. Some of the content that organizations use in OPM methodologies are:

◆ Document templates;

◆ Process descriptions, documentation, relationship diagrams, and guidelines;

◆ Role definitions and descriptions;

◆ Project minimum and compliance requirements;

◆ Schedule and time management materials and instructions;

◆ Risk management materials and instructions;

◆ Cost and budget management materials and instructions;

◆ Resource capacity plans;

◆ Instructions for recommended tools (e.g., computer software);

◆ Portfolio dashboard management;

◆ Performance reports;

◆ Gate reviews and health checks;

◆ Sustainability guidelines;

◆ Regulatory standards; and

◆ Change management, process, and tools.

Organizations may also use content specific to their industry sector, business area, and/or organization, including:

◆ Sales and marketing materials and instructions;

◆ Health, safety, and environmental materials;

◆ Information on stakeholders and customers; and

◆ Regulatory and statutory norms and laws.

4.2.1 ESTABLISHING OPM METHODOLOGIES

OPM methodologies can be established in a number of different ways, such as by:

◆ Building on public-domain materials, such as a project management standard;

◆ Building on commercial materials, such as a commercial project management methodology;

◆ Establishing a methodology without relying on public-domain or commercial materials;

◆ Taking advantage of materials from successful project experiences, and

◆ Building on an organization's assets.

Organizations establishing OPM methodologies should:

◆ Identify organizational background, culture, and circumstances likely to affect methodology development and use.

◆ Understand the outcomes expected from methodology use.

◆ Identify already existing (often informal) practices within the organization that contribute to the expected outcomes.

◆ Fit the methodology with the elements most likely to provide expected outcomes.

◆ Populate the methodology with the contents most likely to provide expected outcomes.

◆ Provide guidance for tailoring and applying the methodology to specific project contexts.

Building an OPM methodology based on public domain or commercial materials offers several advantages over building a specific methodology for the organization. Some of these advantages are:

◆ Standard/methodology principles, elements, and contents have been developed by subject matter experts;

◆ Standard/methodology principles, elements, and contents are recognized nationally and/or internationally; and

◆ Standard/methodology principles, elements, and contents are updated regularly.

Despite these advantages, some organizations prefer to establish an OPM methodology without relying on public-domain and/or commercial materials. These organizations may perceive their projects to be so unique that a standard approach would not provide adequate results. With appropriate tailoring and application, most organizations achieve good results with OPM methodologies built on public-domain and/or commercial materials.

4.2.2 TAILORING AND APPLYING OPM METHODOLOGIES

All OPM methodologies require tailoring as part of the development work through which they are established and as part of the ongoing work through which they are maintained. Tailoring refers to the development work through which OPM methodologies are enhanced to better fit the organizational background, culture, and circumstances and to better provide the expected outcomes.

At the time an OPM methodology is established, tailoring ensures that (a) an appropriate foundation is selected on which to build the methodology and (b) the appropriate methodology elements and contents are selected to achieve the expected outcomes. Unless appropriate tailoring is carried out when the OPM methodology is established, the resulting methodology is likely to be limited in its ability to provide the expected outcomes.

As part of the methodology maintenance process, tailoring ensures that the methodology elements and contents are maintained and enhanced so that the methodology continuously provides the expected outcomes and fits the organizational backgrounds and circumstances. Without appropriate tailoring, the resulting OPM methodology may not provide the expected outcomes for the long term, regardless of how well it has performed.

Tailoring OPM methodologies typically ensures alignment with organizational backgrounds and circumstances. However, tailoring is seldom able to provide methodologies that fully fit the needs of specific projects. Portfolios, programs, and projects should be permitted to apply the OPM methodologies in ways that best fit the specific needs of projects, within boundaries. Applying OPM methodology may include activities such as adjusting methodology features (e.g., tools, techniques, and ways of working), which are considered fit for purpose. Determining how OPM methodology is applied should occur during the planning phase of a project.

4.3 KNOWLEDGE MANAGEMENT

Knowledge management is a concept involving an organization's deliberate and focused attention to generate, collect, organize, analyze, and disseminate its knowledge in terms of documentation, resources, and people skills. Knowledge management involves a process of providing information combined with context to enhance decision making and the ability to take action. It is important that the knowledge management approach is aligned with the defined OPM model in order provide consistency in execution and delivery according to the OPM principles defined in Section 1.3.1.

4.3.1 KNOWLEDGE MANAGEMENT FOR OPM

OPM is the integration of people, knowledge, and processes, and is supported by tools across functional domains of the organization. OPM supports the appropriate balance across people, knowledge, and processes combined with supportive tools to deliver its portfolio, program, and project management efforts. Within the OPM framework, knowledge management typically focuses on organizational objectives such as:

◆ Improved performance,

◆ Innovation,

◆ Sharing lessons learned,

◆ Documenting best practices,

◆ Process integration, and

◆ Organizational continuous improvement.

4.3.2 ORGANIZATIONAL OBJECTIVES

The main objective of knowledge management is to enable organizational learning on an ongoing basis. Organizational learning leads to increased understanding and the addition of relevant knowledge. Organizational learning is based on acquiring knowledge from the situations and their outcome. In the context of organizational project management, additional objectives for organizational learning can include the following:

◆ **Improved performance.** Refers to the delivery of project outcomes that meet expectations and realize the intended value. This includes the performance of people, systems, processes, and tools.

◆ **Advancement.** Refers to the solicitation, incubation, prioritization, and project execution of ideas to support the advancement of organization's targets and objectives.

◆ **Sharing lessons learned.** To enhance knowledge management and the effectiveness of organizational project management, capturing lessons, analyzing impact, and adopting changes are critical to the future value OPM can provide.

◆ **Integration.** Refers to incorporating OPM knowledge management efforts in alignment with the overall organization's knowledge management focus. There needs to be some level of alignment to avoid noncompliance or contradictions.

◆ **Organizational continuous improvement.** Knowledge management should focus on continuous improvement, ensuring that the learning journey is constant and the evolution of knowledge management is increasingly embraced across the organization.

4.3.3 KNOWLEDGE MANAGEMENT LIFE CYCLE

In order to obtain the benefits outlined in Section 4.3.2, knowledge management should cover a complete knowledge management life cycle (see Figure 4-1). This life cycle covers the inception of knowledge up to the moment when the knowledge is successfully applied to benefit actual initiatives within the organization (see Figure 4-1). Knowledge management should focus on three aspects.

◆ **Documentation.** This is the documentation required to support OPM knowledge enhancement. This may be documentation that already exists or needs to be created. Examples include current documentation, new documentation, documentation storage, and documentation updates.

◆ **Resources.** These are resources needed to deliver training, create supporting documentation, make updates and help guide users on knowledge needed. Examples include trainers, creators of documentation, owners of documentation updates, and creators of user guides.

◆ **Individual learning.** This refers to individuals enhancing their knowledge, which is required to ensure the success of organizational project management. Examples include training, tools, processes, and measure improvements.

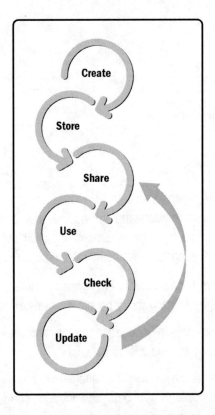

Figure 4-1. Knowledge Management Life Cycle

4.3.3.1 CREATE KNOWLEDGE CONTENT

When establishing knowledge management in support of OPM, an assessment is recommended to determine existing information that can be leveraged and to identify gaps where capabilities need to be created. Knowledge creation is critical to support the transition and ongoing value that OPM provides to an organization.

Existing assets could include tacit and explicit knowledge. This knowledge comes from the way that portfolio, program, and/or project management has been taking place. When not documented explicitly, this would exist as tacit knowledge which needs to be extracted as part of knowledge creation and used in subsequent phases of the knowledge management life cycle.

4.3.3.2 SHARE KNOWLEDGE CONTENT

Knowledge sharing is about making the appropriate knowledge available to the appropriate people, in the appropriate time, in the appropriate mode, and in the appropriate frequency. Individuals seeking specific knowledge should be able to articulate what they need. There should be an effort to inform individuals that the knowledge exists and provide guidance on how to leverage and apply.

4.3.3.3 STORE KNOWLEDGE CONTENT

Knowledge should be stored and organized in a central repository that is easily accessible by the appropriate people. The objective is to organize information in a way that meets the needs of the organization and guide users to where the information is available.

4.3.3.4 USE KNOWLEDGE CONTENT

The use of knowledge management is critical to the advancement of OPM and the value of the knowledge created. It is important to guide employees on how to leverage the knowledge management assets, provide guidance on which learnings to apply, and share knowledge with others.

4.3.3.5 UPDATE KNOWLEDGE CONTENT

Knowledge management assets should be maintained regularly to reflect the evolution of the OPM model and organizational needs. When knowledge management assets are not maintained, behaviors will revert and inconsistencies will surface as employees seek other knowledge inputs. Maintaining updates to knowledge management assets through ongoing feedback supports more consistency across the organization.

In addition, OPM should clearly communicate knowledge gaps and set clear expectations where queries and suggestions are encouraged so that assets can be created or enhanced. Conversely, outdated assets should be removed.

4.3.4 BEST-IN-CLASS LEARNING ENVIRONMENT

Creating a best-in-class learning environment is the foundation of an organization's journey toward realizing the benefits of OPM. This type of learning environment includes:

◆ Creating a demand for information and knowledge,

◆ Easy access and navigation of information sought,

◆ Well-written procedures and/or training videos and other materials and tools that enhance the learning process and can be used as personal learning environments for stakeholders,

◆ Opportunities and environments to practice what is being taught,

◆ Opportunities to collaborate in a dedicated community with subject matter expert involvement, and

◆ Organizational support for the application of knowledge, which reinforces behaviors and encourages the desire for continuous learning.

4.3.5 MEASURING IMPACT OF KNOWLEDGE MANAGEMENT

Measures should focus on business results. The organization should identify metrics that can actually be measured and select the top three to five items that directly support OPM strategy. Measuring current state performance and reassessing to determine the journey and pace at which the organization is embracing learnings is a valid metric that reflects organizational maturity.

4.4 TALENT MANAGEMENT

Most organizations have a process for assessing and providing feedback on the performance of individuals. In many organizations, this is performed by a centralized function. This function tracks the professional development of the project management community and may or may not be linked to promotion and/or compensation review processes. Organizations often use this process to ensure that they attract and retain the appropriate staff.

Assurance is needed to determine that the organization's review process is aligned with, and not in conflict with, the professional development of the portfolio, program, and project managers. This is especially important when seeking feedback on performance in relation to the organization's review cycle and process. The feedback sought and captured should be such that it can demonstrate evidence that competence is being applied.

An organization's promotion process should be synchronized with the requirements defined for the job role and job level. Any existing process needs to be considered and amended in line with the respective responsibilities, experience, knowledge, skills, and education that are required by the organization. It is a good practice to seek evidence of competences being demonstrated prior to authorization of a promotion. Further details to support this can be found in the *Project Manager Competency Development Framework* [4].

When considering how to implement a talent management or competency framework for project management within an organization, a number of factors should be considered, including the following:

◆ **Current and future needs.** The organization needs to understand and recognize what its future talent requirements are and the associated competences. The organization can develop a roadmap in order to respond to these requirements.

◆ **Country and political factors.** These include work councils and local legislation or legal requirements.

◆ **Mentoring and coaching.** Where organizations already have a mentoring and/or coaching approach, it needs to be aligned with the project management requirements.

◆ **Training and development.** An organization will need to integrate its portfolio, program, and project management training and development approach with the training and development approaches in place for other disciplines. A role-based training curriculum can prove valuable in helping to guide individuals to the most appropriate training for not only for their current needs, but to support their career aspirations.

- ◆ **Culture.** The importance of cultural sensitivities should be considered.

- ◆ **Continuous improvement.** This is essential for the ongoing growth and development of the project management community of practitioners.

4.4.1 ASSESSMENT (FORMAL OR SELF-ASSESSMENT)

In order to understand what an individual's development needs are and also to see where an individual may be able to act in the role of coach and/or mentor, an assessment method is required. This can be either (a) a self-assessment, which is a formal assessment where feedback is gathered from those who work with or manage the individual, or (b) a capability assessment administered by an external third party. Many organizations use a 360-degree assessment in which feedback is sought and gathered from peers and team members in addition to managers. However, it should be noted that there are limitations to this method, as less-experienced team members or peers may not be able to comment on the development needs of someone more experienced.

Where a third-party assessment is used, it should be properly and effectively introduced by human resources, the organization's training division(s), or the capability development department. This ensures that the vendor clearly understands the organization's processes, people, work practices, and assets. This also ensures inclusivity and a structured approach when developing and managing the assessment process across the organization. The assessment should be established to ensure that program and project teams have the skills necessary to deliver the program or project and that long-range competency needs are met.

4.4.2 COMPETENCY DEVELOPMENT PLANS

Once feedback has been gathered either from the individual by means of a self-assessment, an assessment from others, or a combination of both, it is essential that the appropriate development activities are identified and that the individual and/or the organization undertakes the identified development activities.

The results of the assessment should be addressed in a timely manner, as there may be items identified by the assessment that warrant immediate corrective action. Furthermore, the competency development plan should prioritize areas to be addressed that are most critical to the individual and the organization. Once the areas have been prioritized, a realistic timeline for the plan needs to be established.

There are various ways of addressing the development needs of an individual. These can include experiential learning, formal learning, and informal learning. Usually the competency development plan will include a combination of these approaches. Each of these approaches is described in the following sections.

4.4.2.1 EXPERIENTIAL LEARNING

Experiential learning is the act of learning by doing or through practice, which allows individual portfolio, program, or project managers to address many of their development needs on the job. Experiential learning can include:

- ◆ Mentoring/coaching,
- ◆ Peer-to-peer coaching,
- ◆ Role playing,

- Simulation/gamification,

- Reflective practices,

- On-the-job-training, and

- Job shadowing.

4.4.2.2 FORMAL LEARNING

Formal learning is a structured approach to education delivered either through traditional instructor-led classroom learning, book-based learning, web-based learning, a technology platform, virtual learning, peer-reviewed publications, or electronic educational database learning. Examples of formal learning include:

- Classroom training,

- Instructor-led virtual training,

- Computer-based training,

- External public training, and

- Blended learning (i.e., a combination of computer-based and classroom learning).

4.4.2.3 INFORMAL LEARNING

Informal learning is a method of learning that occurs in a natural way outside of traditional formal education programs. The following are some informal learning activities that may be beneficial to a portfolio, program, and project manager's development:

- Seminars, conferences, workshops, and forums;

- Web and video conferences;

- Face-to-face meetings;

- Audio and soft-copy books;

- Hard-copy books and peer-reviewed journals and periodicals;

- Podcasts;

- Blogs;

- Online discussion forums;

- Networking through various relevant domain-specific communities of practice (online or face-to-face);

- Professional, statutory, and regulatory body publications; and

- Project management communities and social network websites.

4.4.3 JOB ROLES AND DESCRIPTIONS

An organization needs to establish and maintain its own job function structure aligned with the roles within the organization. For example, some organizations choose to split the project manager role into a number of levels.

These could be levels one, two, and three, where level three is considered to be an experienced or senior project manager. Similarly, this applies to portfolio and program managers. The various levels and specific roles are determined by the types, size, and complexity of the portfolios, programs, and projects being managed. An individual's level can be determined by experience, combined with an assessment (see Section 4.4.1) and feedback on performance. Job roles and descriptions should also include clear definitions of the following, but not limited to:

◆ Reporting relationships among managers and subordinates,

◆ Delegation of duties, and

◆ Responsibilities for rules and procedures.

It is a common practice to associate and align a number of competencies and formal certifications for each job level within the whole project management job code construct. It may be expected, for example, that a project manager should possess a Project Management Professional (PMP)® certification before being classified as a senior project manager or that a program manager would need a Program Management Professional (PgMP)® certification and a portfolio manager would need a Portfolio Management Professional (PfMP)®. The training or competency development framework should be based on the specific skills required by the organization to deliver its portfolios, programs, and projects.

4.5 OPM GOVERNANCE

The alignment between OPM governance and the key principles of OPM is defined in Section 3.5. Governance includes all levels of the organization and may transcend business lines. Governance is not limited to project leadership, but includes representation from any business unit that has impact, influence, or involvement in portfolios, programs, and projects. It provides leadership involvement and support to the performing organization.

OPM governance enables organizations to consistently manage projects and maximize the value of project outcomes. It provides a framework in which organizations can make decisions that satisfy business needs and expectations. OPM governance is achieved through the actions of a review and decision-making body that is charged with endorsing or approving recommendations for the OPM elements under its authority. Consistent with organizational governance, OPM governance practices promote adherence to OPM policy throughout the organization. OPM governance varies based on the business needs of the organization.

OPM governance is a function that is aligned with the executive governance body (vertically and horizontally). It is the management framework within which portfolio, program, and project decisions are made. It is a decision-making framework that is logical, robust, and repeatable and is used to govern organizational assets.

Effective OPM governance supports organizational success by:

◆ Forming clear, well-understood agreements as to the ways a sponsoring organization oversees, contributes to, and supports or aligns portfolios, programs, and projects;

◆ Describing the degree of autonomy and responsibility that individuals are given in the pursuit of the organization's goals;

◆ Ensuring that portfolio, program, and project goals remain aligned with the strategic vision, operational capabilities, resource commitments, and organizational capacity to execute projects and adapt to resulting change;

◆ Creating a set of robust key performance indicators (KPIs) that provides the ability to monitor and review the performance of the organization to support sound business decisions; and

◆ Establishing respective decision-making boards, which ensure that the results delivered through initiatives are aligned with overall benefits realization.

Other core-enabling processes implemented by the organization are integrated with governance through the review and monitoring of process-specific key performance indicators. Recommendations and initiatives are reviewed and accepted using the governance processes, which enhance current processes and methodologies identified during routine assessment reviews.

Depending on how it is defined, OPM governance may have steering committees as part of its structure that will resolve conflicts; change priorities; and terminate portfolios, programs, or projects. In addition, OPM governance may expedite new portfolios, programs, or projects included in initiatives that may not have been considered for a particular strategic cycle. A benefit of steering committees is that their members can view issues from a different perspective to see the cause of a conflict and offer an outside voice of reason.

Governance is not "one size fits all." Depending on the organization, governance may have distinct levels, which are further described in Section 4.5.1. The executive governance level may be the model to follow for OPM governance, which is supported by portfolio and program governance as well as project governance. The level of governance applied depends upon the size, complexity, and criticality of the portfolio, program, or project (see Figure 4-2).

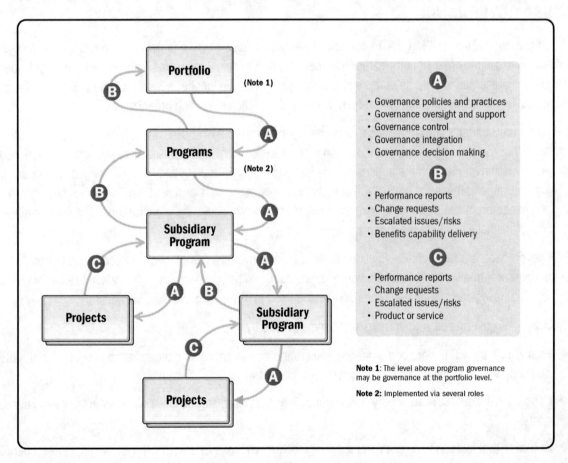

Figure 4-2. Governance Hierarchy

OPM governance assesses a number of factors including but not limited to the areas in the following list:

◆ Prioritization of portfolios, programs, and projects;

◆ Portfolio, program, or project size (e.g., budget, duration, cross-functional versus functional, and team size);

◆ Portfolio, program, or project risk profile (e.g., number of risks, potential impact, probability, and risk status);

◆ Resource requirements (including funding requirements);

◆ Nature of the portfolio, program, or project (e.g., regulatory, strategic, tactical, or operational); and

◆ Interdependencies (e.g., stand-alone, cross-functional, or intrafunctional) teams.

An OPM governance assessment is similar to using a project portfolio management value assessment that may measure revenue growth, employee or customer satisfaction, increased operating margins, enhancement of reputation, or branding.

4.5.1 GOVERNANCE ENTITIES

There can be various governance entities that are dependent on the maturity level and the organizational structure type. These entities could include the following:

◆ **Executive governance entity.** Comprises senior executives and may have board members. It has the responsibility for establishing an open communication channel with the OPM governance body to communicate any strategic changes or portfolio, program, and/or project reprioritization. The need for intervening with the OPM approach when it is ineffective is very important, especially in an organization that is at the bottom of the learning curve.

◆ **OPM governance entity.** Responsible for ensuring that the OPM infrastructure (see Figure 3-1) is always well aligned with organizational strategy and that it is fully operational. This also includes ensuring that all key roles (e.g., portfolio managers, PMO) are properly staffed with skilled people. It also (a) monitors the output from portfolio monitoring processes; (b) reviews the audit results in the areas of portfolio, program, and project management; and (c) regularly interviews key OPM stakeholders (see Section 1.7) to measure their satisfaction and collect suggestions for improvements on both the tactical and strategic levels. It also intervenes whenever an OPM approach or ineffective OPM infrastructure puts the realization of strategic initiatives at risk or causes unnecessary inefficiencies in the organization. This can be critically important for those organizations in the process of defining and adopting an OPM infrastructure. In smaller organizations, this entity could be the same as an executive governance entity.

◆ **Portfolio and program governance entity.** Follows a model similar to the OPM governance body. Portfolio and program managers report on benefits realization and any conflict that requires attention.

◆ **Project management governance entity.** Transmits all the changes from the strategic levels and identifies the impacted projects that may need to reconsider budget, schedule, risks, constraints, or other factors. This role can be performed by the PMO, if one exists, or by a portfolio or program leader.

5

IMPLEMENTATION OF OPM

5.1 INTRODUCTION

In this standard, organizational project management (OPM) initiatives collectively include new implementations or improvements to existing OPM frameworks. These initiatives require a vision as well as agreed-upon strategies and plans to effectively achieve that vision and the strategic objectives of organizational transformation. Senior management sets a vision with the expectation of adding value to the organization through OPM, such as expanded market share, improved service delivery, higher profitability, or agility to respond to rapid changes in the organization's environment. Program management is the recommended domain for delivering an OPM implementation, because (a) it provides the governance structure required to manage the complexity of organizational change that OPM requires; and (b) it provides a focus on benefit realization (adding organizational value) that is necessary for OPM success.

This section focuses on the relevant aspects of OPM implementation initiatives that enable more effective use of both this standard and *The Standard for Program Management* [5]. Used together, these standards help to define and plan an OPM implementation program that delivers the needed capabilities through projects, improve OPM performance outcomes through the transition and use of new/improved capabilities, leverage those improved outcomes to realize the expected benefits of OPM, and finally sustain organizational transformation through post-transition management. Additionally, *Managing Change in Organizations: A Practice Guide* [6] is a useful reference for organizational transformation initiatives such as an OPM implementation.

5.2 DEFINING THE OPM INITIATIVE

Together with the formal aspects of program management defined in standards such as *The Standard for Program Management* [5], several key elements form the foundation for an OPM implementation initiative:

◆ Strategic need for change,

◆ Defined vision from the outcome of change,

◆ Key performance indicators that are used to define achievement of OPM outcomes and to monitor progress toward achievement of the vision,

◆ Current state assessment,

◆ Closure actions for identified capability gaps through OPM implementation project work,

◆ Definition of the target operating model (i.e., future state of the organization),

◆ Proposed business cases, and

◆ Feasibility review to assess OPM improvement potential.

Organizational change initiatives require a significant commitment of leadership and an investment of resources and time as well as buy-in from the organization being transformed. Organizational transformation initiatives can be disruptive, and planning them requires a wide range of resources and operational knowledge to ensure the stability of ongoing operations as change occurs. Planning organizational transformation initiatives also requires the dedication of time and resources as well as the involvement of subject matter experts and other stakeholders.

OPM initiatives can be a complex undertaking; therefore, program definition should be performed using a two-step approach:

◆ **Step 1 Program Formulation.** A high-level view of the program vision and business case is evaluated for feasibility. In program formulation, the OPM initiative is evaluated to determine if it has a desirable business case for the purposes of understanding the potential impacts to the organization, assessing readiness for change, and committing the proper resources and time for detailed OPM planning.

◆ **Step 2 Program Preparation.** A detailed plan where the more detailed work and business case are defined as a baseline for execution. Activities in the preparation stage of the OPM implementation program include the following:

  ■ Establish the OPM implementation program organization, including defined roles and responsibilities.

  ■ Establish OPM initiative program governance.

  ■ Identify the future state capability requirements.

  ■ Perform discovery and analysis (e.g., assessment of the current state against the future state capability model).

  ■ Develop a program management plan for the initiative.

  ■ Prioritize and align initiative component work.

  ■ Develop the OPM implementation roadmap.

  ■ Update/refine the OPM vision and business case.

  ■ Conduct an OPM implementation program plan review.

The originating steering committee (initiating committee) conducts ongoing progress reviews to assess the ongoing viability of the OPM initiative throughout its life cycle based upon the business case risks, environmental factors, and the impacts to ongoing operations.

Sections 5.3 through 5.10 provide recommendations for performing the various activities required to define an OPM implementation program.

5.3 DEFINE ROLES AND THE PROGRAM ORGANIZATION

The need for OPM implementation could be the result of organizational environmental factors such as organizational changes (e.g., reorganization, growth, mergers, or acquisitions), changes in strategic direction, enhanced pressure from competition, regulatory compliance, corporate policies, or market challenges. The need may also arise due to shortfalls in the existing OPM framework or due to earlier attempts to implement OPM that did not deliver the expected outcomes or successful transformation evidenced by benefits sustainment. OPM implementation initiatives also typically involve a significant transformation of the organization's culture, especially in organizations at the initial stages of OPM implementation.

Stakeholder engagement is complex, and ongoing operations should continue without disruption while the organization undergoes change. As OPM initiatives are transformational, effective selection of program governance, sponsorship, and the core program team are important elements for initiative success. To achieve success, in addition to selecting the program organization with the right competency and roles, the most important attributes to be considered in program leadership selection are the proper influence, authority, and control to manage organizational change.

Organizational change should be planned, managed, and realized at a similar level to the technical process aspects of OPM. This concurrent focus on organizational change and OPM process implementation requires a significant amount of stakeholder engagement to adopt the new OPM processes and tools. It also requires an active leadership role within the OPM initiative governance model that participates in defining the requirements that reflect the user's perspective in order to enhance transition, adopt a new way of working, and ensure sustainable benefits realization. In cases where an organizational entity exists that has responsibility for OPM performance, such as a project/program management office (PMO) or organizational excellence function, this department or office may be the logical choice to manage an OPM implementation program. The PMO, however, is typically not the target audience for most of the transformation. The ongoing operations or business-as-usual organization that actually uses the new OPM capabilities should have an active leadership role in planning, execution, and ownership of the transition and benefits realization phases. This is discussed further in Section 5.3.5. An example of an OPM implementation program organization is shown in Figure 5-1.

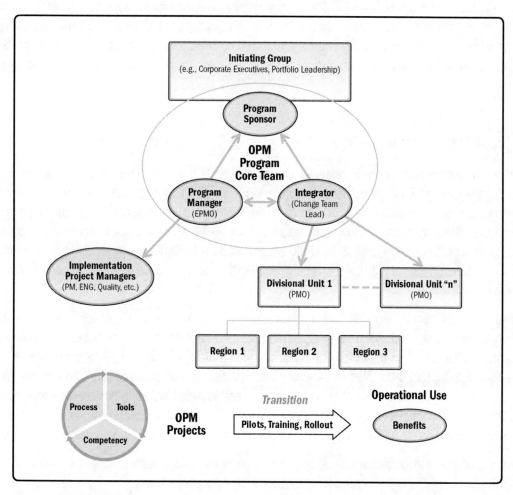

Figure 5-1. Example of OPM Implementation Program Organization, Roles, and Relationships

5.3.1 OPM INITIATING COMMITTEE

Typically, the senior leadership (e.g., corporate executive or portfolio leadership) of the organization staffs the initiating committee or possibly a portfolio management board. The initiating committee establishes programs and projects that facilitate the realization of the organizational strategy. In order to maintain alignment of the OPM initiative with organizational strategy, a member of the initiating committee typically serves as the OPM implementation program sponsor.

5.3.2 OPM IMPLEMENTATION PROGRAM SPONSOR

The OPM implementation program sponsor provides resources and leadership direction for the OPM implementation program and is accountable to the initiating committee for program success. An active, engaged, and visible sponsor is crucial. The sponsor should have the proper organizational authority, resources, and influence to remove barriers and to provide day-to-day guidance to ensure success of the OPM implementation. Because program management involves the delivery of new capabilities and required transition activities, programs often encounter complex challenges that include resource limitations, technical challenges, and resistance to change. As an example, a shortfall in resources can limit the scope of capabilities delivered by the component projects, which may in turn limit the full realization of planned benefits. Further, if resistance to change arises, the new capabilities may not be adopted or may not be sustained, which reduces the value of implementing them. In this case, the role of the sponsor involves both justifying the allocation of resources to the initiating committee as well as influencing the adoption of new OPM capabilities by the target organization undergoing organizational change. The sponsor is also responsible for sustaining benefits realization.

5.3.3 PROJECT MANAGEMENT OFFICE

The term PMO used here generically refers to an organizational entity (see Sections 1.6.2 and 1.6.3) that is responsible for the OPM governance framework and performance that supports portfolio, program, and/or project management functions for an entire organization (e.g., an EPMO) or a unit/function within the organization. The PMO in an organization may be the entity that defines and maintains the process governance framework related to portfolio, program, or project management. The PMO may also be the implementer or recipient of OPM governance, since there may be many types of PMOs within an organization that differ in scope, authority, reporting hierarchy, and responsibilities.

Depending on organizational needs, culture, and structure, the PMO may operate on an enterprise (i.e., EPMO), business unit, divisional, or functional level (e.g., IT, research and development, or marketing). There may also be specific-purpose PMOs based on the emergent needs of the organization. For example, a temporary PMO may be formed specifically to support the implementation of an enterprise resource planning (ERP) system. An ERP is used to collect, store, manage, and interpret data from many business activities including human resources and financial processes. The establishment of a temporary PMO may highlight the need for a structured and formalized governance framework where none existed. A PMO may support OPM implementation in the following ways:

◆ Provide guidance and subject matter expertise regarding the processes and tools for managing portfolios, programs, and projects in the organization as well as OPM maturity models.

◆ Develop organizational governance frameworks, hierarchies, and relationships.

◆ Oversee portfolio, program, and project strategic alignment and facilitate key OPM decisions (e.g., prioritization and resource assignment).

◆ Apply, utilize, and maintain portfolio, program, and project management standards and methodologies.

◆ Establish a project management information system (PMIS) to collect, gather, and integrate OPM information and prepare online reports.

◆ Perform as a center of excellence, which gathers and evaluates industry knowledge and practices in OPM and implements them in a manner that adds value to the organization.

◆ Monitor OPM implementation performance including portfolio, program, and project performance (actual versus planned performance), benefits, and key performance indicators.

◆ Support legal, regulatory, environmental, and financial compliance audits.

◆ Monitor compliance to policies and procedures.

◆ Facilitate organization-wide stakeholder engagement and agreement.

◆ Conduct OPM implementation program quality assurance reviews.

In many cases, a resource from the PMO acts as the OPM implementation program manager based on the individual's ability to manage programs and familiarity with the development of OPM practices, processes, and tools.

5.3.4 OPM IMPLEMENTATION PROGRAM MANAGER

The organization should select an implementation program manager by considering the optimum level in the organization from which the program will be most effectively managed. In complex organizations with extended regional operations or divisions, a central enterprise project management office (EPMO) as shown in Figure 5-1 might provide a program manager to lead the OPM initiative. The program manager is accountable to the program sponsor and is responsible for the planning, execution, and overall management of the OPM implementation. In Figure 5-1, organizational change is taking place in the extended units, and the local/regional PMOs and their practitioners are the elements of the organization most affected by the changes. The local-level PMOs are responsible for the day-to-day execution of projects and will use the new capabilities over the long term to deliver and sustain organizational benefits. The integrator role in the OPM implementation program core team represents the day-to-day operational element of the organization. In a complex organization with multiple locations, the program manager might work with an organizational change lead or integrator who represents the interests of the user community. This role is described further in Section 5.3.5.

5.3.5 OPM INTEGRATOR AND ORGANIZATIONAL CHANGE TEAM

The program organization that implements OPM is temporary. The part of the organization that adopts, transitions, and uses the new OPM infrastructure for the long term is important for stakeholder engagement. For any transformation to be successful, the operational or functional organization should adopt the new way of working by integrating and orchestrating operations in a manner that both realizes and sustains benefits (i.e., adding and sustaining organizational strategic value). The functional leaders who accept, transition, and use OPM capabilities, as well as understand the organization's culture, can provide guidance during the development of requirements for new OPM capabilities and the validation of OPM-targeted benefits. Further, these stakeholders are responsible for managing acceptance and transition, and generating the expected benefits in the sustained future environment. Participation in OPM implementation program leadership enhances buy-in and ownership that is valuable to the OPM initiative's success. An important aspect of organizational efficiency and OPM adoption is achieved by tailoring OPM capabilities and governance to the environment in which they will be applied and used. Since OPM also involves collaboration with other functions of the organization that are outside of the PMO (e.g., procurement, quality, contract management, marketing/sales, field operations, or engineering), their representation on the organizational change team should be considered. The successful integration of these functions is important with respect to organizational benefit realization.

In larger, complex organizations as shown in Figure 5-1, where OPM implementation requires adoption across several organizational units or regions, it is recommended to establish an organization change team. This team should be led by an OPM integrator and have representation from the organization's ongoing operations that will implement and use the OPM framework. In this role, the OPM integrator is responsible for change leadership and representing the various users of the OPM capabilities. In less complex organizations, the integrator role could be a direct representative of the project management or functional line community who will be the primary users of the new OPM capabilities developed by the PMO.

5.3.6 ADDITIONAL ROLES

Depending on the complexity and scope of the initiative, additional roles may be added to support the OPM implementation program. The extent of participation for these roles can range from providing subject matter consultation to part-time collateral duties to full-time assignment. For example, individuals skilled in business analysis may be required in order to support analysis of the as-is and to-be organizational states. Broadly, business analysis is the set of activities performed to support the delivery of solutions that align to business objectives and provide continuous value to the organization (refer to *The PMI Guide to Business Analysis*, p. 9 [7]). These skills can be helpful in both designing the future-state capabilities and also in developing requirements that can be used to charter various projects and other related work within the OPM implementation program. Given the importance of aligning OPM implementation efforts to support the organizational strategies, it may be beneficial to employ resources skilled in (a) eliciting business needs from stakeholders, (b) documenting key stakeholder needs to support development of the OPM business case, (c) analyzing current and proposing future organizational states, and (d) partnering with other members of the OPM implementation team to support implementation success.

5.4 DEVELOP BUSINESS CASE

The business case for OPM implementation is developed by understanding and quantifying the impact of OPM performance as it relates to the strategic objectives of the organization. In short, the business case defines the financial impact to the organization when projects deliver or do not deliver as planned. The business case for OPM arises from two elements: (a) the cost to implement or improve a selected group of OPM capabilities and transition them to improve organizational outcomes, and (b) the benefits from the result of those outcome improvements.

Benefits should be identified by quantifying them in financial terms as much as possible. This enables determination of the return on investment that can be compared to the cost of OPM implementation. For organizations that perform projects infrequently, the investment to develop a high-maturity OPM capability may be greater than the benefit realized from it. For example, an organization whose core offering is service delivery and occasionally performs projects might find that the cost impacts incurred due to additional errors and inefficiency in project management are far less than the cost to establish a rigorous OPM infrastructure. It may make more sense to hire others to manage the project or simply accept the cost of nonconformance errors. However, for organizations that engage in programs and projects as a key enabler for market capture, public service, or to improve their organizational performance, shortfalls in OPM component performance can have far-reaching strategic impacts beyond late delivery or exceeding project budget. Some examples where poor OPM performance can affect organizational value realization include the following:

◆ Projects that overrun schedules often overrun budget in terms of both cost and resource usage, resulting in lower project profit margins.

◆ Poor requirements development may result in numerous change requests, which add cost, delay delivery, and may impact the utilization of project outputs.

◆ Late or poorly planned projects may prohibit the organizational portfolio from achieving its strategic objectives (e.g., total number of project completions for the year) when resources are not available for planned follow-on work.

◆ Late capability or new product delivery within programs delays benefits realization and impacts return on investment and net present value as in missing a market opportunity window.

◆ Delayed projects may have detrimental impacts on customer satisfaction ratings and result in loss of market share or future sales where project delivery dependability is critically important.

◆ Quality suffers when projects are stressed. Rework to fix defects during projects adds cost and time delays. Warranty claims after the delivery of projects erode customer satisfaction, impacting the investment value of the project to both the supplier and the customer. These in turn impact market share or future investments or expose the organization to legal actions.

◆ Poor communication and reporting to stakeholders may add significant risk, for example, in terms of poor or conflicting requirements, work performance management, and managing customer expectations.

From a benefits management perspective, it is important to understand the relationship between OPM capabilities, expected outcomes from the use of those capabilities, and the benefits realized from the improvement of those outcomes. Outcomes are the result of performing a capability and are the desired changes that are related to the implementation of the OPM capability. These outcomes are desired because the organization can leverage them to realize benefits. The performance of the new process should be evaluated against the quality of its expected outcomes as well as the additional effort and time required to perform it. This helps to fully understand whether the new process is adding value over what existed previously or simply adding overhead effort, time, and cost. For example, when the new project planning process improves outcomes (e.g., more predictable delivery to plan, reduced project execution cycle time, reduced errors, or improved project quality), then it will likely deliver benefits (e.g., reduced rework/recovery costs, improved project profit and improved portfolio performance). These also may improve stakeholder satisfaction and brand recognition that can deliver benefits such as improved sales, greater market share, or higher quality services.

Intangible benefits should also be assessed and quantified where possible. Outcomes, such as improved employee satisfaction, may be detected through surveys and may be measurable in terms of employee retention, attendance, and productivity. A favorable place to work often attracts the best talent and retains them. A further discussion of OPM performance metrics is addressed in Section 5.8.

Examples of areas affected by OPM performance that can be considered in a business case as potential benefits are:

◆ Customer satisfaction,

◆ Market share capture,

◆ Impacts to internal or customer programs as a result of project delivery performance (e.g., time-to-market impacts to net present value),

◆ Brand recognition,

◆ Portfolio effects (e.g., conducting more projects per year than planned),

◆ Project profit margin,

◆ Employee productivity,

◆ Employee satisfaction and retention,

◆ Risk exposure,

◆ Competitive ranking,

◆ Market expectations regarding OPM performance,

◆ Organizational scaling (e.g., organizational growth),

◆ Life-cycle time reductions,

◆ Warranty and liabilities cost reduction (cost of quality), and

◆ Efficiency improvements through the mitigation of high-demand periods.

Further benefits are realized as OPM maturity improves. Establishing defined and measured processes enables process optimization methods that may be applied repeatedly across other programs and projects in the organization. Examples include improvements in process cycle time or value contributions of processes, and reduction of workflow delays.

In summary, a business case for OPM improvement focuses on the elimination of waste, reliable delivery to plan, and impact to the expected value at the portfolio and program level. Higher OPM maturity enables organizations to more confidently engage in challenging endeavors and adapt to change. Because projects are investments, the expected benefit from the utilization of their outputs is typically far greater than the cost of the project. The impact of OPM performance on the return of that investment in projects is considered as part of the strategic value of OPM improvement.

5.5 OPM MATURITY

OPM maturity is the level of an organization's ability to deliver desired strategic outcomes in a predictable, controllable, and reliable manner. OPM maturity influences the OPM implementation program in three aspects:

◆ **Future State.** Consists of defining the OPM capability that will enable delivery of the organization's strategic objectives and quantify the progress of the program towards that state;

◆ **Business case.** Provides cost to establish and sustain the targeted level of OPM maturity as well as the benefits of improving OPM outcomes and organizational performance.

◆ **Program roadmap.** Defines the evolution pathway for OPM maturity development of the organization from the current state to establishing and sustaining the future state including any planned intermediate stages.

OPM models define specific requirements for each increment of OPM maturity and assessment tools for the measurement of organizational progress toward the planned maturity target (see Section 5.6). Some models assign numerical levels of organizational maturity. One example includes maturity levels 1 through 5 where level 1 represents an organization with little or no defined OPM process structure and level 5 represents an organization with a high degree of data-driven processes with effective organizational capabilities. Other models focus on the maturity of the OPM capabilities themselves (e.g., standardized, measured, controlled, and continuously improved). In this example, specific capabilities may be selected for maturity development that fit the organization's OPM maturity strategy.

The following list provides generic descriptions of the characteristics of OPM maturity levels. Although the descriptions describe projects, they could also apply to portfolios and programs. Exact definitions of each level varies among OPM models and should be a consideration when selecting an OPM model to follow as to whether the maturity levels or stages fit the transformation strategy and culture of the organization.

◆ **Level 1—Initial or ad-hoc.** Project performance is not reliably predictable. Project management is reactive and is highly dependent on the experience and competency of the people performing the work. Projects are completed but are often delayed, over budget, and quality varies. OPM processes, where they exist, are ad hoc and chaotic.

◆ **Level 2—Project-level adoption of OPM.** Projects are planned, performed, monitored, and controlled at the project or functional level following generally accepted practices. However, OPM processes and practices are not uniformly applied or managed from an organizational perspective and may vary from project to project. Functional departments, such as procurement or design engineering, may have institutionalized processes to guide work in their departments, but those processes may not be aligned with project operations.

◆ **Level 3—Organizationally defined OPM.** Project management is proactive and organizational project performance is predictable. Project teams follow organizationally established OPM processes that are tailored to the complexity of the projects and the competency of practitioners. OPM processes are organizationally standardized, measured, controlled, and can be analyzed by the organization to monitor and control OPM process performance.

◆ **Level 4—Quantitatively managed OPM.** Project management decisions and process management in the organization are data-driven. OPM process performance is managed in a manner that enables the achievement of quantitative improvement objectives. OPM process performance is systematically analyzed for improvement opportunities that add value to the organization (e.g., enhance benefits at an acceptable cost).

◆ **Level 5—OPM optimization.** The organization is stable and focused on continuous improvement. The alignment of OPM to the organizational strategy, coupled with defined and measured OPM processes with a focus on value contribution, fosters organizational agility and innovation. In an optimized organization, implementation of continuous improvement has been established along with a robust set of measures and metrics. The success rate of programs and projects is high, and the portfolio is optimized to ensure business value. Projects are selected for their impact on the strategy of the organization.

In order to establish the level of organizational maturity that is needed, a comparison of the organization's current state with industry benchmark data and stakeholder requirements is recommended. The current state of OPM maturity is typically determined through an OPM maturity assessment using an OPM model. Benchmarking data may be obtained from market or industry surveys or through professional research organizations.

Even though the highest maturity level in any given model is a notable achievement, resources are not infinite. The organization often needs to focus scarce resources to achieve the level of maturity that keeps the organization ahead of its competitors and meets or exceeds market and stakeholder expectations. Additionally, the OPM implementation should consider the organization's ability to manage change. Many maturity models offer an ability to measure the maturity level for a given capability or Knowledge Area. Organizations may take this tailored approach to fine-tune specific OPM capabilities whose outcomes have the greatest effect on beneficial goals and expectations.

Although OPM maturity objectives vary among industries and organizations, a common objective for OPM implementation is to select a maturity level in the middle of the range (level 3 or organizationally defined OPM in the previous example) since this usually represents an organization that exhibits OPM capabilities that are standardized, tailored, measured, and consistently implemented. A level 3 organization applies OPM with the proper rigor and has its "finger on the pulse" of the organization's project performance. The data collected can then be evaluated (a) to establish the business case to improve capability areas that are not delivering outcomes as expected or (b) to optimize capabilities that enhance the organization's competitive advantage and the time and effort of internal resources. Having an established OPM governance framework with OPM performance data readily available and under constant review sets the stage for enhancing organizational agility when the operational or market environment changes.

After the targeted level of maturity is identified, OPM models can be consulted to evaluate recommendations for specific practice implementation as well as process governance, maintenance, and required control infrastructure. Because the future state is defined to be capable of delivering these targets, the cost of resources to conduct the component projects and related work comprises the cost side of the OPM implementation business case. These costs are compared with the expected benefits related to the organization's transformation from the current state to realize the OPM implementation vision (e.g., delivering to plan or exceeding market expectations).

5.6 DEFINE THE ROLE OF OPM MATURITY MODELS IN THE INITIATIVE

OPM maturity models are often cited as tools for measuring an organization's adoption and consistent implementation of recommended practices in project management. *A Guide to the Project Management Body of Knowledge* (*PMBOK® Guide*) – Sixth Edition [8] defines a best practice as the methods currently recognized within a given industry or discipline to achieve a stated goal or objective. As it relates to higher maturity, a best practice is a recommended practice that is proven effective and delivers value to the organization that implements it. The usual sources for these recommended practices are global standards.

OPM maturity models leverage two foundational concepts in their constructs:

◆ Recommended practices specific to and in support of portfolio, program, and project management. In some models, this may also include enabling functional practices that support these initiatives (e.g., systems engineering, procurement, and contract management) and organizational enablers (e.g., competency management, information management, and governance).

◆ A prescribed pathway to achieve capability or process maturity (e.g., institutionalization, effectiveness measurement, tailoring, control, performance monitoring, process analytics, and optimization). In the context of OPM maturity models, this may include organizational enablers that support OPM.

With respect to organizational transformation, people tend to use and support things that add value to either their own lives or the organization they support. They tend to reject or avoid things that don't add value. The organization needs to know that the OPM processes are being followed, but also that those processes are delivering the expected value.

A practical example of how OPM maturity models interact with an organization's governance and project environment is shown in Figure 5-2.

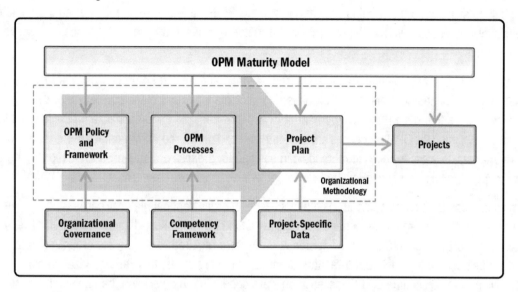

Figure 5-2. Example of OPM Maturity Model Interaction in a Project Organization

An OPM maturity model is a capability excellence model for evaluating an organization's project management processes and supporting infrastructure. Organizational policies play a key role, because they define the organizational need for OPM processes and set the culture and guiding principles of the organization. Policies are the rules and guidelines formulated by senior management to be adopted by an organization and are typically published in a manner that is widely accessible. Policies and procedures are designed to influence and determine major decisions and actions, as well as all activities that take place within the boundaries set by them. In comparison, procedures are the specific methods employed to execute policies in the day-to-day operations of the organization. Together, policies and procedures ensure that a point of view held by the governing body of an organization is translated into steps that result in an outcome that complies with that view. Typical examples of policies are: safety, security, data confidentiality, and employee travel policies. An OPM policy should express senior management's commitment to the implementation and improvement of its OPM governance system.

Organizational policies underpin the authority for expending resources on OPM processes and supporting infrastructure and are the foundation upon which the organization builds its capabilities. Policies also establish the requirements for OPM process and infrastructure development In the early stages of OPM maturity development, even as the formal OPM processes are being set in place, the policies define senior management's expectation for what needs to be performed, thus providing executive buy-in and the basis for organizational change.

To aid in consistent compliance with the framework policies, OPM processes are established for portfolio, program, and project management practitioners and stakeholders. Another important consideration is the level of detail required for each process. The appropriate level of detail relies heavily on the competency development of the process user and the degree of project complexity. The level of process detail is sufficient when it is understood by the user and provides a sufficient amount of rigor to deliver the expected outcome.

Project complexity should also be considered. For example, to ensure risk management for small, frequent projects, a list of typical risks encountered with recommended actions to be taken by the project manager may be sufficient.

This risk register may be the result of the evaluation of many of the organization's projects by a PMO. For a large, complex program or a project, a risk management workshop with subject matter experts, including sophisticated tools and tracking systems for performing the various aspects of risk management, may be required. The extent to which the organization has arrived at the correct level of detail is measured in the OPM process effectiveness and compliance metrics.

When an organization has developed institutionalized, tailored, and measured processes, this forms a foundation upon which project management plans can be based. Project management plans can leverage the organization's policies and processes to reduce plan development time and effort as well as to capitalize on the lessons learned of the organization. Because the OPM processes are standardized and measured, OPM process performance metrics are available for analysis. Process excellence methods can be used for process effectiveness evaluation, identification of improvement opportunities, and continuous improvement where a business case exists.

One aspect of many OPM maturity models is that each level of organizational maturity carries with it some required specific practices that an organization demonstrates as standardized, tailored, and measured. The processes, organizational support infrastructure, and competency framework required to enable the organization to deliver the expected benefits become the desired future state or target operating model that the organization plans to develop. As stated previously in this standard, OPM assessments are conducted to determine the gaps in the current state of the organization, and efforts to close these gaps become OPM implementation program work components.

Many OPM maturity models provide guidance on establishing measurement and analysis of OPM processes for both compliance and effectiveness. These metrics are critically important, because as new processes and practices are established, the organization needs to be capable of knowing that the processes are being used and are adding the expected value. Processes that are not adding value may be contributing to the overhead burden and will need to be optimized or eliminated. The focus on added value and the promotion of a data-driven, learning organization foster an organizational environment that is capable of adjusting to market or operational changes. A state of defined and measured processes as well as alignment with value contribution enable process improvement methodologies.

OPM maturity models typically also provide some guidance or means to measure the OPM maturity of an organization. This is useful to establish a current state baseline for OPM maturity, identify OPM capability gaps, and verify progress towards the OPM maturity goal. An OPM assessment is (a) a compliance audit of OPM capabilities against a recommended standard or governance framework and (b) an evaluation of the effectiveness of the OPM capability in achieving the performance outcome that satisfies the organization's operational and strategic requirements. It is the performance outcomes of OPM capabilities that enable organizational benefits of OPM. An independent expert assessment of the organization's current state should be conducted whenever feasible. This assessment will establish an OPM maturity baseline against which OPM capability implementation or improvement progress can be planned and compared. The progress of improving the OPM maturity against OPM outcome performance can be measured against the OPM performance baseline discussed in Section 5.9.

5.7 PROCESS MANAGEMENT

Process management is the application of knowledge, tools, techniques, and systems to define, perform, measure, control, report, and improve processes. There are practices in an organization that represent what people actually do (behavior) and documented processes that define the actions or activities that management is directing them to perform. Documented processes may include procedures, policies, work instructions, workflows, checklists, or guides. They may be contained in a separate written procedure or embedded as directions in a computer program or application.

When considering organizational maturity, a fundamental tenet is that process management is in place. Formal process management ensures that practices are more easily and consistently communicated, measured, controlled, and improved. Maturity in process management ensures that the organization has defined processes that are institutionalized, repeatable, and measured. It also ensures that (a) the organization is aware of how effectively processes deliver their expected outcomes, (b) the processes are efficiently performed within an acceptable period of time, and (c) the value contribution of those processes is achieved. Processes that are not performed effectively and efficiently or do not enable the value expected of them should be challenged. Higher maturity in process management provides a structured culture for innovation, process improvement, and organizational agility.

Figure 5-3 depicts the supportive and dependent relationship between processes, technology, and competency. For example, the level of process detail and process effectiveness is dependent upon the level of competency of the user. If a competency development system is not in place in an organization, processes should be written with additional detail so that users of all skill levels are able to effectively follow them. When a competency system is in place, more succinct processes with prompts or a checklist might be sufficient to ensure consistent implementation. Tools and technology may establish a standardized process by controlling the process actions as well as capturing process information and workflow, allowing proper process tailoring, ensuring process compliance, and measuring process effectiveness.

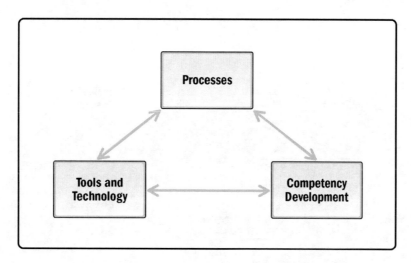

Figure 5-3. The Relationship Between Competency Development, Tools and Technology, and Processes.

5.8 ESTABLISH OPM PERFORMANCE METRICS AND KEY PERFORMANCE INDICATORS

As part of the OPM implementation roadmap, an entity that is responsible for OPM performance metrics, quality, and key performance indicators (KPIs) should be established and used to assess an organization's strategic alignment. To the extent practical, this entity should look outward at threats and opportunities on the horizon that could impact the organization's performance. At the organizational level, a balanced scorecard that shows a balance of financial and nonfinancial KPIs should be established. A balanced scorecard is critical to assessing the health and performance of an organization. KPIs are used to assess whether expectations are clearly defined and accountabilities are aligned with strategic priorities. KPIs can also be used to measure personnel commitment to or understanding of an organization's vision, mission, and objectives. Additional KPIs can be implemented (a) to ensure that the organization's efforts and rewards are aligned and (b) to assess management of the portfolios, programs, and projects. For example, an organization could establish a KPI to assess management by measuring the number of portfolios, programs, and projects reviewed using the organization's OPM control and decision process. Care should be taken to avoid too many KPIs, which may result in misalignment or incompatibility of the KPIs within an organization.

Added value can be realized by establishing an organizational entity responsible for the continued maintenance and governance of the OPM performance system. This can be part of another function (e.g., part of the quality assurance department) or can be a dedicated group such as a PMO or a center of excellence. This entity should be established early in the program so that the responsible staff members are part of the full life cycle of the OPM implementation. The members would also be responsible for maturing and improving the OPM performance system.

High-level OPM performance metrics can be developed by evaluating variances with respect to the project performance measurement baselines (PMB) for cost, schedule, and scope. These evaluations should occur at key review points across the project management life cycle as depicted in Figure 5-4. The key decision points across the project life cycle of a customer-facing project may be described as the "as sold" (project initiation), "as planned" (project planning), "as built/delivered" (project delivery), and "final" (project closeout). At these points, the cost, schedule, and scope including forecast data are evaluated for changes from the previous phase as part of the project monitoring and controlling process.

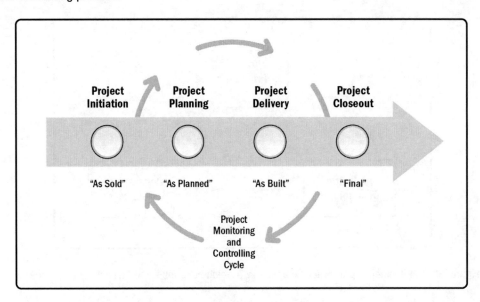

Figure 5-4. Project Performance Measurement Baseline (PMB) Comparisons at Specific Instances Throughout the Project Life Cycle.

In ideal high-maturity organizations, the forecast and actual project performance metrics will match the baseline established at project initiation (e.g., as sold to the customer in the case of an external project, or as committed to senior management in the case of internal projects). This reflects that there were no or minimal changes to scope (stable and exact requirements), high-quality estimates, risks that are perfectly managed through execution, adequate resources, and high-quality deliverables with no issues in the post-delivery phase (close-out). Of course, this is the ideal case. In reality, even high-maturity organizations experience projects that do not perform as planned (e.g., "black swan" events). However, high-maturity organizations learn from these shortfalls.

In low-maturity organizations, these baselines reveal where problems and errors arise in projects as well as the effectiveness of the organization's governance framework for managing projects. For example, if the baseline set as a result of project planning does not agree with the project initiation baseline, there is a question regarding the quality of the performance in the previous stage. Further, if the performance at the end of project delivery does not align with the approved baseline for project planning, there could be a concern with how the project work was executed or whether the planning process was deficient. Differences between the project delivery and project closeout phases could reveal that although the project completed on budget and schedule, quality may have been sacrificed and additional cost could be incurred after project delivery during the warranty phase. Errors found in the warranty or field operational phase are not only significantly more costly to remedy, but also can have a significant effect on customer satisfaction and repeat business. When planning an OPM improvement initiative, consideration should be given to the impact of detecting, fixing, or eliminating these errors as early as possible in the program or project life cycle.

Therefore, organizations may focus on the early stages that have a greater impact on project error reduction, cost, and design stability. Some examples of OPM process performance that can be evaluated by measuring their process outcomes are listed below:

◆ Effective requirements development results in fewer changes to scope and drives any changes to requirements as early in the project life cycle as possible. This minimizes the cost of the change as well as schedule and quality impacts. Effective requirements development also has an impact on customer and employee satisfaction (less redundant or wasted work).

◆ Effective risk management reduces threat exposure and the effects of uncertainty. The effectiveness of a risk management process can be measured by the accuracy of the planned allocation of risk contingency resources or budget. A risk contingency that is too high requires funding and resources that could have been allocated to other projects in the portfolio (e.g., executing fewer projects per year than strategically desired). If the risk contingency for a project is too low, unplanned threats and risk responses that arise will require additional budget. This may require a reduction in other project budgets within the organization's portfolio, raising portfolio risk exposure and delivery uncertainty.

◆ OPM governance framework effectiveness can be measured in terms of project delivery reliability (delivery to plan predictability), project life-cycle duration/cost, market impacts, organizational profitability related to project performance contribution, and the effect of project delivery execution on portfolio/program benefits realization.

As discussed in Section 5.4, intangible benefits should also be considered for assessment and financial impacts. In many cases, intangible benefits are measured by indirect methods such as surveys, improved employee satisfaction, and brand recognition. These intangible benefits can have positive impacts on employee productivity and may help to attract and retain the best talent. Organizations that deliver projects more successfully with less rework tend to be viewed more positively not only by the customer, but also by the organization's employees.

In summary, an OPM implementation program performance measurement baseline should consider the initial, current, and expected future state target for: (a) planned OPM capabilities (e.g., the OPM process framework), (b) the performance outcomes of the OPM capabilities, and (c) the planned benefits that are related to the OPM performance outcomes. It is also important that the organization defines and measures the expected outcomes that will be changed by the implementation of new or improved OPM capabilities. The OPM performance measurement baseline is the basis for an OPM implementation program dashboard.

5.9 PLANNING CONSIDERATIONS FOR THE OPM INITIATIVE

OPM initiatives do not always follow a straight path to completion. Depending on the amount of change that an organization can manage at any given time, an iterative approach may be used where some OPM implementation is done, but the outcomes and acceptance are evaluated to determine the work performed in the next phase or sequence of implementation. A new way of working often benefits from piloting and follow-on work. This helps to improve OPM adoption where the implementation is adjusted based on lessons learned from the early stages of the program. Planning directly to the end in a prescriptive manner may not be feasible. Using iterative controlled stages of OPM implementation that target specific process outcomes and can be leveraged for incremental benefit may be required to realize quick wins and progressive success. One example is to improve the processes for project initiation first, because these early stages of a project may be the least costly to implement and may yield stability in the project performance later in the project life cycle. Quick wins to gain stakeholder buy-in and validate the decision by management to implement OPM are highly encouraged. At each phase of the OPM implementation program, the business case should be evaluated for viability. This is important because as benefits are realized or adjusted, new benefits are identified and the effectiveness of transformational change may impact the resources and direction needed to achieve the desired vision. Additionally, OPM performance should be carefully monitored to understand when OPM implementation is sufficient. It is not unusual to embark on a journey to reach a level 5 maturity to discover that level 3 satisfies the organization's strategic objectives and market expectations.

Implementing or improving OPM maturity is not a short or single-cycle event—it typically involves a significant amount of organizational change. This is especially relevant in low-maturity organizations, which have been enabled traditionally by individual skills and techniques rather than organizational processes. The best OPM framework is not effective at delivering organizational value if people do not use and adopt the new practices. Trust needs to be developed, the rate of change should be controlled, and good practices in organizational change management should be applied.

Improving from one maturity level to another is generally a 1- to 2-year endeavor and is resource-intensive. The organization should plan only for the amount of change that it can accommodate. Over the course of an OPM implementation program, the internal and external environments often change as a result of factors such as reorganization, mergers, acquisitions, and market trends. The information in this section together with *The Standard for Program Management* [5] and *Managing Change in Organizations: A Practice Guide* [6] will be useful to mitigate uncertainty and to understand and effectively implement transformational change.

6

ONGOING OPM MANAGEMENT AND MONITORING

6.1 INTRODUCTION

This section addresses how the organization can ensure that the organizational project management (OPM) initiative successfully realizes the planned benefits and that the benefits are sustained after the implementation program is completed. It also discusses (a) how long-term monitoring of the implemented OPM system is performed to ensure that it continues to deliver benefits and (b) how to continue to improve the OPM system. The monitoring of the implementation program itself is not addressed as it is covered in *The Standard for Program Management* [5].

As explained in Sections 2 and 5, studies have shown that the majority of organizations that do not pursue continued improvement will regress and lose the value previously attained. For that reason, it is important to ensure that the OPM initiative includes a continuous improvement process.

6.2 ENSURING OPM BENEFITS REALIZATION AND SUSTAINMENT

Benefits realization and sustainment are key to OPM implementation program success. There are two phases associated with OPM management and monitoring. The first phase is during the program itself and soon after the capabilities are delivered to the organization and adopted by the users. The second phase follows the closeout of the program and involves long-term monitoring and measurement.

In a program, benefits begin to be realized as the program and its projects transition from project completion (ready for rollout) and are handed over to the operational unit. Completion of a project is not a benefit; rather, the use of the project's output (the outcome) should achieve a benefit. Management and monitoring of these individual benefits is important to ensure that the benefits have been achieved and to ensure that no unintended negative outcomes have resulted from the change.

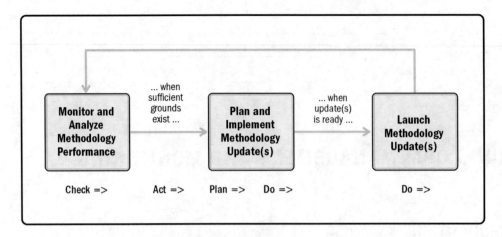

Figure 6-1. OPM Methodology Maintenance Process—Long-Term Model

Figure 6-1 shows a long-term model for overall OPM methodology monitoring and management. Organizations plan and put in place the structure to perform this monitoring and improvement to ensure that (a) the OPM system continues to provide value and benefits to the organization and (b) the benefits can be optimized on a long-term basis.

As the detailed implementation plan is carried out and OPM is incorporated into the organization, the organization begins to realize the intended benefits as defined in the benefits realization plan. In order to determine whether the intended OPM organizational benefits are being realized, the OPM implementation team measures progress according to the defined quantitative key performance indicators (KPIs).

Measuring the business impact from an OPM implementation is the best way to show business leaders the value of an OPM implementation. This is also the most challenging metric to incorporate. Business leaders are interested in business results that affect the bottom line, such as time to market, budget attainment, resource utilization, and other metrics that directly measure the organization's attainment of its strategy. For example, it may be possible to take a project management-specific indicator, such as the increase in projects completed on time, and associate it with a business value indicator (e.g., time to market), to determine a financial value to the business.

For any new program or initiative, sustainability is commonly an issue, whether it is OPM improvement, total quality management (TQM), Six Sigma, a new human resource (HR) initiative, or the use of an enterprise system. It is important for the organization to ensure that the new initiative is sustained and the identified benefits are realized. A large cross-functional improvement like OPM impacts many organizations so it is difficult to involve all stakeholders in its maintenance. It is recommended to implement some form of PMO and establish executive sponsorship.

For OPM implementation programs to succeed, the operational organization should:

◆ Own the new capabilities.

◆ Ensure that the outcomes of their usage by everyday users meet expectations.

◆ Ensure that those outcomes continue to deliver the benefits (benefits realization) and add value to the organization.

◆ Communicate to the organization's stakeholders about the successes from the program, including any internal or external customer experiences.

6.3 LONG-TERM MONITORING AND ANALYSIS OF OPM

Monitoring and analyzing methodology performance aims to keep track of the methodology service (i.e., the extent to which the methodology satisfies the expectations that organizations have regarding the methodology) and to collect proven practices and lessons learned. Organizations may establish KPIs, use Six Sigma, and use lean procedures to analyze methodology performance. KPIs are recommended for ongoing governance and process maintenance. Examples of KPIs include cycle time (i.e., time to execute portions of work) and effectiveness.

Monitoring and analyzing methodology performance comprises the following elements:

◆ **Monitoring methodology use.** The aim is to understand how and to what extent the methodology is used, including identifying the methodology sections that are not being used or are being utilized incorrectly, and the reasons for this. This monitoring should also look at stakeholder satisfaction with the methodology.

◆ **Monitoring methodology results.** The aim is to understand how and to what extent the methodology is providing the expected results, including identifying any shortcomings in the methodology and the reasons for them. The KPIs for the processes will be used for this effort.

◆ **Analyzing methodology performance.** The aim is to understand the effectiveness of the methodology. This may take place by analyzing the methodology use, methodology results, or both, and should tie back into the planned benefits and value to the organization and the business case.

◆ **Collecting and analyzing project management experience.** The aim is to collect and analyze new experiences from practical projects, and to understand how these experiences may be recycled to enhance project effectiveness, efficiency, and chances of project success.

◆ **Collecting and analyzing project management knowledge.** The aim is to collect and analyze new knowledge from project management research and development and to consider how it may be used to enhance project effectiveness, efficiency, and chances of project success. This may take place by following project management books, journals, and conference papers, as well as updates to the public domain and commercial project management methodologies by the methodology providers.

◆ **Strategic alignment.** The aim is to ensure the alignment of the project related portfolio(s) with the organizational strategy to maximize the portfolios' contribution to the strategic goals. With the implementation of OPM, effectiveness is increasingly measured by how clearly the project management function can map a direct line back to the success of the overall organizational performance.

Monitoring and analyzing methodology performance may take place continuously, at regular time intervals, or as required. Similarly, monitoring and analyzing of methodology performance may take place on several parallel tracks and at several different levels. An organization may:

◆ Collect lessons learned and gather information on recommended practices and OPM knowledge continuously.

◆ Collect a methodology maintenance backlog for medium-range methodology updates.

◆ Update a methodology when new public domain and commercial project management methodology platforms are released by the relevant providers.

When sufficient grounds exist for a methodology update, the next step in the methodology maintenance cycle is initiated without interruption of monitoring and methodology performance analysis.

6.4 PLANNING AND IMPLEMENTING METHODOLOGY UPDATES

Planning and implementing methodology updates aims to provide the methodology updates considered necessary by relevant bodies. These steps are briefly described as follows:

◆ **Initiating methodology updates.** Updates may take place through the OPM methodology development team, the BAU organizations, the PMO, or another body. The concept is to make a well-founded decision regarding (a) whether sufficient grounds exist to start a methodology maintenance cycle and (b) which methodology sections, if any, require updating.

◆ **Planning and implementing methodology updates.** These may take place as a process or as a project. The idea is to implement the updates as identified by the authorized body. Initiating, planning, and implementing methodology updates takes place as with any project. Some organizations expect the maintenance project to pilot the methodology updates as they are being initiated, planned, and implemented in order to prove their usability and added value to the organization and its projects.

6.5 LAUNCHING METHODOLOGY UPDATES

Launching methodology updates includes the need to inform project management staff and project stakeholders of the changes to the methodology structures, contents, and reasons the methodology is changing or being introduced. This may take place continuously as new methodology elements are available, or in major launches. The idea is to communicate clearly what was updated, why it was updated, who is impacted by the update, and how the methodology was updated.

Launching methodology updates is a critical part of the methodology maintenance cycle. Even the best methodological concepts may be incorrectly understood and ignored unless they are appropriately communicated and explained, and their use encouraged and expected.

APPENDIX X1
CONTRIBUTORS AND REVIEWERS OF *THE STANDARD FOR ORGANIZATIONAL PROJECT MANAGEMENT*

X1.1 CORE COMMITTEE

The following individuals were members of the Core Committee responsible for drafting the standard, including adjudication of reviewer comments.

Norman K. Prevost, PMP, Committee Chair
Dave Gunner MSc, PMP, Committee Vice Chair
Joseph A. Sopko, MS, PMP, MSP, Committee Vice Chair
Christopher Edwards, MBA, PMP
Craig Letavec, PfMP
Amy J. Martin, MBA, PMP
Conrado Morlan, PfMP, PMP
Glenn Strausser, MBA, PMP
Jouko Vaskimo, DSc (Tech), PMP
Karl F. Best, PMP, CStd, Standards Specialist

X1.2 REVIEW TEAM

The following individuals were members of a review team who provided content for and review of specific sections of the standard.

Tony Appleby, MBA, PMP

Emad E. Aziz, PfMP, PMP

Panos Chatzipanos, PhD, Dr EUR ING

Samuel YK Cheung, MBA, PMP

Karen Dickson

Kenji Hiraishi, MsE, PMP

Chris Lawler, MEd, PfMP,

Mansoor Mohammed, PfMP, PMP

David A. Maynard, MBA, PMP

Burkhard Meier, MBA, PMP

Jose Angelo Pinto, PMP

Mark N. Scott, PMP

Grzegorz Szalajko, CISA, PMP

Gerhard Tekes, PMP, PMO-CP

Thomas Walenta, PgMP, PMP

X1.3 SUBJECT MATTER EXPERT (SME) REVIEWERS

The following individuals were invited subject matter experts who reviewed the initial draft and provided recommendations for improvement.

Hossam Dib Al-Wazzan, PMP, PMI-RMP

Elias Aziz, PMP, CSM

Claudia M. Baca, PMP

Manuel F. Baquero V., MSc, PMP

Maria Cristina Barbero, PMP, PMI-ACP

Gregorio Bulnes Castro

Jaime Andres Salazar Cabrera, PfMP, PMI-RMP

Graham Campbell

Pietro Casanova, PMP

Panos Chatzipanos, PhD, Dr EUR ING

Cătălin-Teodor Dogaru, MBA, PMP

Louis Duchesne, MPM, PMP

James Duggan, PMP

Wayne D. Ellis, PE, PMP

Algin Erozan, MSc, PMP

Theofanis Giotis, PhD, PMP

Leonid Gomberg, PMP

Mrinal Goswami, MBA, PMP

Poonam Gupta, PMP, MCA

Mustafa Hafizoglu, PMP

Akram Hassan, PhD, PMP

David Hess, MBA, PMP

Hilary Miller Hetzel, MBA, PMP

Kenji Hiraishi, MsE, PMP

Gheorghe Hriscu, PMP, CGEIT

Mohamed Khalifa, PfMP, PgMP

Kimberly Jo Killian, MAAS, PMP

Saneesh Kumar Pothera, MBA, PMP

Hagit Landman, MBA, PMP

Ricardo I.Guido Lavalle, PgMP, PMP

Chris Lawler, MEd, PfMP

Tong (James) Liu, PhD, PMP

Donnie MacNicol, MICE, MAPS

Jan Mandrup

Mansoor Mohammed, PfMP, PMP

Chris Mauck, PMP

Harvey Maylor, PhD

David A. Maynard, MBA, PMP

J. Scott McKinney, PE, PMP

Lourdes Medina, PfMP, PMP

Burkhard Meier, MBA, PMP

Werner Meyer PhD, PMP

Vladimir Antonio Mininel, PMP

Christy L. Minshall, PMP, CMQOE

M. Aslam Mirza, MBA, PMP

Alison K. Munro, MSc, PMP

Alexandre Nabuco, PMP

Daud Nasir, PMP, LSSBB

Andrea Peruzzi, PfMP, PMP

Yvan Petit, PhD, PMP

Jose Angelo Pinto, PMP

Raju N Rao, PMP, SCPM

Thiago Regal, PfMP, PMP

Terry Ricci, PfMP, PMP

Jason Rodrigues, PMI-RMP, MLARM

Shankar Sankaran PhD, PMP

Sachin Saundattikar, MS, PMP

Paul E. Shaltry, MA, PMP

Cindy C Shelton, PMP, PMI-ACP

Nitin Shende, PMP, PBA

Gary J. Sikma, PMP, PMI-ACP

Vijay S Somannavar MBA, PMP

Marcos Rogerio de Sousa, LLM, PMP

M. Sundar, MSc, PMP

Grzegorz Szalajko, PMP, CISA

Michael Thompson

Michelle Venezia, PMP, PMI-ACP

Dave Violette, MPM, PMP

Thomas Walenta, PgMP, PMP

Kim Wells PE, PMP

X1.4 PUBLIC EXPOSURE DRAFT (PED) REVIEWERS

The following individuals participated in the public review of the standard, and provided recommendations for improvement.

Habeeb Abdulla, PMP, RMP

Khalid Saleem R. Abdallah, EMBA, PMP

Taiwo Abraham, MBA, PMP

Srinivasu Adapa, MBA, ITIL

María José Aguilar, MEng, PMP

Phill C. Akinwale, PMP, OPM3

Shaghayegh Aldaghi

Imad Alsadeq, MSc, PMP, P3M3

Abdulrahman Alulaiyan, PMP, PMI-ACP

Hossam Dib Al-Wazzan, PMP, PMI-RMP

Mark A Annunziata, Sr., CGC, PMP

Tony Appleby, MBA, PMP

Syed Rehan Ali Baaqri, PfMP, PgMP

Claudia M. Baca, PMP

Ganesan Balaji, BE, PgMP

Manuel F. Baquero V., MSc, PMP

Shantanu Bhamare, PMP, LIMC

Nigel Blampied, PE, PMP

Kiron D. Bondale, PMP, PMI-ACP

Farid F. Bouges, PhD, PfMP, PMP

Epifanio (Jun) Bucao, AB, PMP

Patsy A. Butler, MHRD, CAPM

Armando Camino, MBA, PMP

Panos Chatzipanos, PhD, Dr EUR ING

Williams Chirinos, MSc, PMP

Sergio Luis Conte, PhD, PMP

Adam D. Coombs, PE, PEng

Mario Coquillat, PMP, PMI-RMP

Cristian Martín Corrales, MPM, PMP

Farshid Damirchilo, MSc, PMP

Gina Davidovic, PgMP, PMP

Jean-Michel de Jaeger, EMBA, PMP

Panini Deshpande, MBS, PMP

Vahid Dokhtzeynal, PMP, PMI-RMP

Wae K. Elmetwaly, PMP, PMI-ACP

Luis Alberto Flores, PMP, PMI-RMP

Eng. Marius Gaitan, PMP

Ivo Gerber, PgMP, PMI-ACP

Theofanis Giotis, PhD, PMP

Kalyani Govindan, PMP

Gabrielle Bonin Haskins, PMP

Mahmoud Mohamed Hassaballa, PMP, AVS

Sergio Herrera-Apestigue, PMP, P3O

Kenji Hiraishi, MSE, PMP

Gheorghe Hriscu, PMP, CGEIT

Shuichi Ikeda

Marcelo Takashi Ito, PMP, PSM I

Ashok Jain, PMP, CSM

Md Javeed, BE, PMP

Kenichi Kagaya, PMP

Oswin Newton Kakumanu, MBA, PgMP

Elias Kassaye Gebregziabher, PRINCE2

Suhail Khaled, PMP, PMI-ACP

Taeyoung Kim, PMP

Jörg Klein, PhD, PMP

Henry Kondo, PMP, PfMP

Rouzbeh Kotobzadeh, PMP, PMI-ACP

Rakesh Kumar, MBA, PMP

Thierry Labriet, PMP

Boon Soon Lam

Adeel Khan Leghari, PgMP, PMP

Tong (James) Liu, PhD, PMP

Ivan Lloro, MSc, PMP
M V Rasa Manikkam, MBA
Jon McGlothian, MBA, PMP
Lourdes Medina, PfMP, PMP
Lubomira Mihailova, MBA, PMP
M. Venkatram Vasi Mohanvasi,
    BE, PMP
Nathan Mourfield, MBA, PMP
Syed Ahsan Mustaqeem, PE, PMP
Mickey Nakamura, PMP, CSM
Marvin R. Nelson, MBA, SCPM
Nghi Nguyen
Kimberly S. Nix, MBA, PMP
Birgit Nothnagel, PMP
Habeeb Omar, PfMP, PgMP
Mozhgan Pakdaman,
    PMP, PMI-RMP
Sue Paquette, PMP
Chen Pengzhi, MSC, PMP

Héctor A. Pérez Zelaya, PMP, MBE
Truc Pham, PMP, PMI-RMP
Crispin "Kik" Piney, PfMP, PgMP
Svetlana Prahova, PMP
S. Ramani, PfMP, PgMP
Santhi Rao
P. Ravikumar, PgMP, PMP
Alexander V. Revin, PMP
Terry Ricci, PfMP, PMP
Dan Stelian Roman PMP, PMI-ACP
Fernando Romero-P, MBA, PMP
Rafael Fernando Ronces Rosas,
    PMP, ITIL
Omar Mohamed Sallam, PMP,
    PMI-RMP
Aminu Sarafa Oluola, PMP, MNSE
Arun Seetharaman, MBA, PMP
Gary J. Sikma, PMP, PMI-ACP
Marisa Silva, MSc, PMP

Mauro Sotille, PMP, PMI-RMP
Mario Špundak, PhD
Chris Stevens, PhD
Shoji Tajima, ITC, PMP
Tetsuya Tani, PMP
Gerhard Tekes, PMP, PMO-CP
Micol Trezza, MBA, PMP
Mai Anh Tyagi, CSM, SASM
Ali Vahedi, PfMP, PgMP
S K Vickram
Dave Violette, MPM, PMP
J. Steven Waddell, MBA, PMP
Gorakhanath Wankhede,
    PMP, MCSE
Muhammad Waseem
Kevin R. Wegryn, PMP, PfMP
Michal P. Wieteska, PMP
Kenichi Yoshida, PMP, ITC

X1.5 PMI STANDARDS MEMBER ADVISORY GROUP (MAG)

The following individuals are members of the PMI Standards Member Advisory Group, who provided direction and input for the standard.

Maria Cristina Barbero, PMP, PMI-ACP
Brian Grafsgaard, PgMP, PMP
Dave Gunner, PfMP, PMP
Hagit Landman, MBA, PMP
Vanina Mangano, PMP, PMI-RMP
Yvan Petit, PhD, PMP
Chris Stevens, PhD
Dave Violette, MPM, PMP
John Zlockie, MBA, PMP, Standards Manager

X1.6 CONSENSUS BODY

The following individuals are members of the Consensus Body, who provided final approval for publication of the standard.

Nigel Blampied, PE, PMP
Chris Cartwright, MPM, PMP
John Dettbarn, DSc, PE
Charles Follin, PMP
Dana Goulston, PMP
Brian Grafsgaard, PgMP, PMP
Dave Gunner, PMP
Dorothy Kangas, PMP
Thomas Kurihara
Hagit Landman, PMP, PMI-SP
Tim MacFadyen, MBA, PMP
Mike Mosley, PE, PMP
Nanette Patton, MSBA, PMP
Yvan Petit, PhD, PMP
Kik Piney, BSc, PgMP
Mike Reed, PfMP, PMP
David Ross, PgMP, PMP
Paul Shaltry, PMP
Chris Stevens, PhD
Geree Streun
David J. Violette, MPM, PMP

X1.7 PMI PRODUCTION STAFF

Donn Greenberg, Manager, Publications
Roberta Storer, Product Editor
Barbara Walsh, Publications Production Supervisor
Kim Shinners, Publications Production Associate

APPENDIX X2
ORGANIZATIONAL CONSIDERATIONS
FOR OPM IMPLEMENTATION

There are a number of aspects that need careful consideration prior to embarking on OPM framework. It is not just a case of one size fits all. When looking at the approach to take with regard to methodology, it is important to analyze and assess what is important to the business. It may be that the business values speed of delivery more than cost or reliability. In this case, the methodology selection needs to ensure that the path taken is the most appropriate one. Similarly, governance requires a holistic view of the organization in order to understand factors such as the culture and needs of the customer (i.e., internal or external customers). Again, the process for managing knowledge is also important, and there needs to be an understanding and appreciation as to how knowledge is currently retained and passed on. Finally, the organizational processes surrounding the development and growth of the project management community should not be overlooked.

X2.1 ASSESS CURRENT STATE AND READINESS

One of the initial steps in the process is to assess the current state from an organizational perspective and determine readiness to proceed. In some cases, the organization may have the desire to proceed; however, it may not be in a position to do so.

The objective is to get a common understanding of the current project management practices within the organization, which creates the foundation for the OPM methodology. This assessment phase consists of the following steps:

◆ Determine whether the organization needs to develop an OPM methodology. Projects may or may not be a major part of the organization's business.

◆ Review the organization's current maturity in the area of project management. This step involves the assessment of the project management maturity and readiness level of the organization.

◆ Evaluate the organizational structure. The reason many organizations perform poorly in project management is not because they have bad project managers or project management practices, but it is because the organizational structure may not support the execution of the projects. This involves looking into areas such as project budgets, resource ownership, and job descriptions.

In order to be able to choose the best starting point for developing or tailoring an OPM methodology, organizations need to identify and consider relevant organizational and project issues, as well as capabilities expected from an OPM methodology. Awareness and consideration of these key issues enables each organization to choose the most effective and efficient methodology foundation that best fits its organizational and project needs. These issues may be assessed with or without a situational assessment tool.

The key is to ensure that the OPM methodology is established in such a way that the result addresses the relevant organizational and project issues. For this reason, it is necessary to understand the backgrounds and circumstances in which an OPM methodology will be operated in. It is also important to improve comprehension of the outcomes that the OPM methodology is expected to provide. It is critical that the OPM methodology fits the organizational and project contexts, backgrounds, and circumstances.

Some of the organizational issues to be considered before attempting to establish an OPM methodology are:

◆ Isolation between organizational business area(s);

◆ Lack of adaptation to national and local traditions and cultural aspects;

◆ Lack of organizational maturity (including project management maturity);

◆ Organization client position(s) (internal/external);

◆ Lack of communication of organizational strategies and tactics;

◆ Lack of agility to adopt organizational trends and pressures toward projects and project management;

◆ Significant issues or areas requiring attention from an organizational point of view; and

◆ Lack of support from key organizational stakeholder(s).

Some of the project issues to be considered before attempting to establish an OPM methodology are:

◆ Projects do not align with the organizational strategy;

◆ Project selected are not enablers to achieve strategic goals;

◆ Poor project governance;

◆ Lack of project roadmap;

◆ Lack of agility to readjust project scope due to internal/external impacts to organizational strategy;

◆ Inability to classify projects by type, application area, or size;

◆ Lack of prioritization of project risk(s);

◆ Strict project life cycle;

◆ Inability to manage project deliverable complexity;

◆ Lack of skilled resources to manage project pace; and

◆ Lack of support from key project stakeholder(s).

Some of the reasons to support the development of an OPM methodology are:

◆ Providing a common way of working,

◆ Providing structure to projects,

◆ Standardizing projects and providing consistency,

◆ Providing a common project language and/or vocabulary,

◆ Enhancing the quality of project management,

◆ Recirculating lessons learned and best practices,

◆ Enhancing OPM,

◆ Enhancing project risk management,

◆ Enhancing project schedule management,

◆ Enhancing project scope management,

◆ Enhancing chances of project success,

◆ Enhancing project effectiveness, and

◆ Enhancing project efficiency.

By considering these issues, and by taking them into consideration when establishing, developing, and maintaining an OPM methodology, an organization is more likely to develop a methodology that fits organizational and project contexts, backgrounds, and circumstances, and provides the expected results.

Another major consideration when selecting a methodology for the organization, is the importance on how quickly a methodology needs to be in place, in relation to how complex the projects and programs are. Figure X2-1 illustrates that with complex programs or projects, the processes, tools, and methodology need to be tailorable, wherever possible, for each program or project. If the programs and projects are simple with few complexity factors (human, system or ambiguity), it is recommended to adopt a simple approach or methodology. For additional information on complexity, refer to *Navigating Complexity: A Practice Guide* [9].

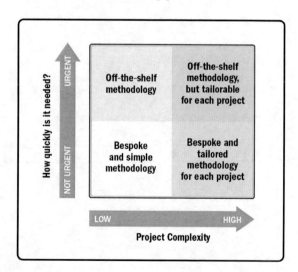

Figure X2-1. Priority Assessment—What is Important to the Organization

APPENDIX X3
RECOMMENDED SURVEY QUESTIONS REGARDING IMPLEMENTATION OF OPM INITIATIVES

The survey questions contained in this appendix are intended to help an organization perform a self-assessment to determine where it stands with regard to implementation factors associated with OPM. This survey is designed for organizations in the foundational or improvement stages. It is not intended to be an exhaustive or restrictive list, but rather guide users to typical critical implementation considerations. Another approach is to conduct a more formal assessment using *Organizational Project Management Maturity Model (OPM3®)* [10] and related services.

X3.1 QUESTIONS RELATING TO IMPLEMENTATION OF CRITICAL SUCCESS FACTORS

X3.1.1 SUSTAINED LEADERSHIP

- ◆ Who is the most senior, appropriately qualified person to sponsor a program fostering OPM?
- ◆ Who is the most senior, appropriately qualified person to lead OPM initiatives on a daily basis?
- ◆ What leadership network across the organization is best positioned to serve as a governance group or steering committee for OPM?
- ◆ What relevant current sponsorship practices are in place?

X3.1.2 CONTINUOUS IMPROVEMENT

- ◆ What actions does the organization take to keep track of the achievements in organizational strategy? What success criteria are used?
- ◆ Who in the organization keeps track of the achievements in organizational strategy?
- ◆ How does the organization identify areas that need to be improved?
- ◆ How does the organization manage risk?
- ◆ Who in the organization defines the contingency plans?
- ◆ How does the organization identify opportunities (internal/external) that may help to achieve organizational strategy?

◆ How does the organization identify threats (internal/external) that may affect the achievement of organizational strategy?

◆ How often is a gap analysis conducted and when was the last one performed?

◆ Who in the organization defines the actions to be taken to achieve the organizational strategy?

◆ How are the organization's continuous improvement activities related to portfolios, programs, and projects?

X3.1.3 ORGANIZATIONAL CHANGE MANAGEMENT

◆ Do the business functional areas work in silos?

◆ How do the business functional areas in the organization perceive the support functions?

◆ How do the supporting functional areas in the organization perceive the business functional areas?

◆ What is the general perception of the supporting functional area?

◆ What is the general perception of the business functional area?

◆ Does the organization have cross-business functional area initiatives?

◆ Have the cross-business functional area initiatives been successful in the organization?

◆ What was the level of involvement of supporting functions in cross-functional initiatives?

◆ Does the organization link initiatives with business processes?

◆ How do projects fit into the cross-business initiatives in the organization?

◆ How do projects fit into the business processes?

◆ How does the organization manage change?

◆ Who leads change management in the organization?

◆ Does the organization have a change management process or policy?

◆ What communication channels exist for each type of stakeholder? How effective are these channels?

X3.2 QUESTIONS RELATING TO GENERAL READINESS FOR OPM INITIATIVES

◆ **Business results.** What is the current performance of contributing portfolios, programs, and projects?

◆ **Environmental factors.** How do the projects resonate with competitors, customers, or regulators?

◆ **Organizational culture and style.** What is the prevalent decision-making model? Is communication informal or formal? What is the organization's tolerance for risk? How results-oriented is the organization? What are the policies and practices relating to how employees are treated and encouraged to develop?

◆ **Organizational experience with substantial improvement changes.** How well does the organization handle change? Is the organization agile when it comes to change? What competing change initiatives could interfere with an OPM initiative?

◆ **Organizational process assets.** What is the governance process related to portfolios, programs, and projects? How does enterprise risk management fit within the context of OPM? How effective is the project management information system? What other management systems require consideration?

◆ **Organizational strategic planning.** Is there a clear bridge from strategy, vision, and mission to the organization's programs and projects?

◆ **Organizational structures.** What are the existing related organizational structures or policies directing structure that may help or hinder an OPM implementation? Is the organization considered to be functional, matrix, or project centric?

◆ **OPM-related roles and responsibilities.** Are there PMOs in place? Is there a formal or informal community of project management practice?

◆ **Previous organizational project management assessment results.** What credible knowledge exists regarding current capabilities and performance results relating to portfolios, programs, and projects?

◆ **Stakeholder list.** Who are the people in the organization that need to be on board for an OPM initiative? What will it take to get them there?

X3.3 QUESTIONS RELATING TO THE IMPLEMENTATION OF CORE-ENABLING PROCESSES

X3.3.1 STRATEGIC ALIGNMENT

◆ Does the organization have a documented strategic plan? Is it visible in yearly business plans?

◆ Do the business functional areas of the organization start projects independently without consulting the senior management team?

◆ Do all business and supporting functional area heads understand the purpose of the organization?

◆ How integrated are the business and supporting functional areas in the organization?

◆ Does the organization understand the benefit of aligning business and supporting functional areas to achieve the purpose of the organization?

◆ Do the heads (i.e., manager/director/vice president) of the supporting functional areas understand what the business functional areas do for the organization?

◆ Do the heads (i.e., manager/director/vice president) of the business functional areas understand what the supporting functional areas do for the organization?

◆ Do the employees of the organization understand what the supporting functional areas do for the organization?

◆ Do the employees of the organization understand what the business functional areas do for the organization?

X3.3.2 ORGANIZATIONAL PROJECT MANAGEMENT METHODOLOGY

◆ What is the level of project management knowledge in the business functional areas?

◆ What is the level of project management knowledge in the supporting area functions?

◆ When working together, do the business and supporting functional areas in the organization have a holistic approach to engaging portfolios, programs, and projects, or do they focus on their own areas of expertise?

◆ Does the organization have a documented project management methodology of practices and techniques?

◆ What is the project management team's level of experience?

◆ Does the organization have a project management office? What services does it provide?

◆ How does the organization define success and failure metrics for projects?

X3.3.3 GOVERNANCE

◆ Who in the organization approves major projects, for example, general manager/CEO, business functional area head (i.e., manager/director/vice president), or approval committee?

◆ Does the organization have a governance model/framework inclusive of portfolios, programs, and projects?

◆ If so, does the governance model/framework cascade through the business and supporting functional areas?

◆ If not, who in the organization identifies variances in the achievement of the organizational strategy?

◆ How often does the organization review the milestone achievements of the organizational strategy?

◆ Who belongs to the governance entity in the organization?

◆ How often does the governance entity meet?

X3.3.4 COMPETENCY MANAGEMENT

◆ Does the organization have formalized training and development plans for the business and supporting functional areas that support portfolio, program, and project management?

◆ Does the organization have a career development framework for the business and supporting functional areas that includes portfolio, program, and project management?

◆ How do the business and supporting functional areas share lessons learned that relate to improving the quality or efficiency of portfolios, programs, and projects?

◆ Does the organization support the creation and development of OPM-related communities of practice?

◆ How does the organization assess the skills of the management team and employees, related to portfolios, programs, and projects?

◆ Who in the organization is responsible for the professional development of the management team and employees in the areas of concern to OPM?

APPENDIX X4
HOW TO DEVELOP A TAILORED ORGANIZATIONAL PROJECT MANAGEMENT (OPM) METHODOLOGY

X4.1 INTRODUCTION

Organizational project management (OPM) methodology is a system of practices, techniques, procedures, and rules used by those who perform portfolio, program, and project work to meet requirements and deliver benefits. This methodology covers all levels and facets of performing projects, regardless of form, in an organization. It is the heart of the OPM concept because it connects critical parts of the organization. The other core-enabling processes facilitate putting the right project management methodology in place. An effectively tailored methodology makes appropriate and useful connections and modifications with the business model of the organization. The result is a tailored project management methodology with the flexibility to adjust to future needs and changes within the organization.

All organizations are unique as demonstrated by their different objectives, cultures, business models, values, organizational models, strategic drivers, processes and procedures, and internal and external constraints (e.g., regulations). Even organizations that share a common business sector implement their strategies differently. OPM methodology works best when it is tailored for effective use within the context of an organization and is aligned to the needs of the business. The methodology is customized and applied to portfolios, programs, and projects based on the needs and experience of the organization and the project. Methodology application or fit varies by organization depending upon the characteristics of the programs and projects it performs.

In this appendix, the example of developing a tailored methodology applies to projects only. Characteristics such as project type, size, and complexity are basic considerations. The following examples demonstrate how these characteristics modify the manner in which the project methodology is applied:

◆ An IT project requires technical testing with other system components. The methodology supports integration activities, stakeholders, and processes.

◆ A facilities project requires the coordination of third-party products and services. The methodology supports third-party management guidance and processes.

◆ A highly complex project requires enhanced monitoring and control methods to ensure tight alignment of all elements. Tailoring of the monitoring and control practices for the required enhanced scrutiny is applicable.

When an organization manages a number of unique types of projects, it should consider developing multiple methodologies. Multiple methodologies provide consistency within the project type and allow the organization to realize the benefits referenced in the *PMI's Pulse of the Profession® In-Depth Report: The Competitive Advantage of Effective Talent Management* study [3]. Examples of different types of projects that may require different methodologies include, but are not limited to, construction, software, aerospace, and pharmaceutical projects.

Project management methodology uses existing organizational process assets to provide organization-specific structure and guidance, which improves the success of project completion. These organizational process assets include policies, procedures, and knowledge bases (such as lessons learned and historical performance information) specific to and used by the performing organization. Additional organizational process assets may include completed project schedules, risk data, earned value data, benefits realization of programs, and aggregated risk management effectiveness of portfolio management. Organizational process assets are inputs to most planning processes and should be integrated in the project management methodology. Project management methodology is a critical component of OPM methodology and should contain specific references and call-outs to these organizational process assets rather than recreating or excluding them. For example:

◆ Human resource management activities should reference organizational human resource policies.

◆ Cost management activities should reference organizational financial control procedures (e.g., time reporting, required expenditure and disbursement reviews, accounting codes, and standard contract provisions).

◆ The use of organization-specific templates or forms (e.g., risk register, work breakdown structure, project schedule network diagram, and contract templates) is expected as part of the project management methodology. It may be necessary to revise and supplement existing organizational process assets as OPM implementation matures.

X4.2 DEVELOPING THE METHODOLOGY

The following process assists an organization in tailoring its project management methodology, which can be used with minor modifications to develop portfolio and program methodologies. Organizations should consider developing a unique methodology for each project type. If there are similarities in the project types, organizations may consider modifying existing project management methodologies to simplify the methodology development process. Regardless of whether an organization is developing its first methodology or expanding upon an existing set of methodologies, these process steps should be followed to ensure no unique aspects of the project type are overlooked.

The simple inputs, constraints, outputs, and resources (ICOR) diagram shown in Figure X4-1 depicts a high-level process that may be used to generate a tailored methodology.

There are several approaches that can be taken to develop a tailoring process. Organizations can consider the following approach described in Sections X4.3 through X4.11 or develop their own approach.

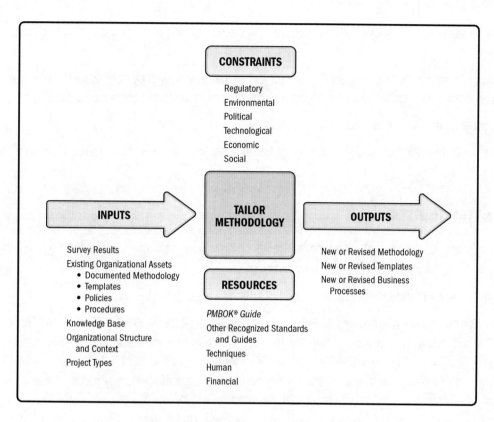

Figure X4-1. Methodology Tailoring Process

X4.3 IDENTIFY TYPES OF PROJECTS

Every organization is unique and needs to determine how to distinguish between project types. To distinguish among project types, ask the following questions:

◆ Are there common lines of business (e.g., construction, aerospace, pharmaceutical) that deliver similar projects?

◆ Are there common levels of risk associated with the project?

◆ Are there varying levels of complexity (e.g., widgets developed in a single location with stable industrial bases vs. international efforts with multiple components that are required to be integrated in order to deliver the project)?

◆ Are there internal and/or external customers?

◆ What is the variance in size of the types of projects performed?

◆ What is the duration of the project?

◆ What is the urgency?

◆ Will the project have significant public or media attention?

◆ Are the project deliverables well-defined or unknown (e.g., building a bridge vs. performing research to test a theory)?

◆ Are the technologies necessary to deliver the project to maturity or do they need to be developed (e.g., building a conventional combustion engine or the next generation of technology for transportation)?

◆ Is the project labor or capital intensive, or both?

◆ Are there any regulatory agencies that need to be involved or regulations that are required to be met?

X4.4 IDENTIFY INPUTS

Identify the inputs to the project management methodology. There are many considerations when tailoring a methodology to a project type, which include the following:

◆ **Results of organizational survey.** Described in Appendix X3 of this standard.

◆ **Enterprise environmental factors (EEFs).** Described in Section 2.2 of the *PMBOK® Guide* [8]. Think "enterprise-wide" when planning and maintaining the project management methodology. Include cross-organization stakeholders (including, but not limited to, human resources, finance, legal, information systems/technology, training, etc.) who can contribute to the development of specific methodology steps or tasks. This is vital to ensure the integration of the business management framework into the project management methodology to achieve the organization's strategic goals and objectives. These cross-organization stakeholders bring the collective knowledge of their areas or business units and offer the detailed and unique perspective that is critical for tailoring a base methodology. Without the addition of the unique characteristics of the organization and its areas/business units, the organization may find little value in the methodology and fall short in its attempt to develop and implement OPM.

◆ **Organizational process assets (OPAs).** Described in Section 2.3 of the *PMBOK® Guide* [8]. Use existing OPAs to provide organization-specific structure and guidance, which improves the success of project completion. OPAs include policies, procedures, and knowledge bases (e.g., lessons learned and historical performance information), specific to and used by the performing organization. OPAs may include completed project schedules, risk data, earned value data, benefits realization of programs, and aggregated risk management effectiveness of the portfolio. OPAs are inputs to most planning processes and should be integrated within the project management methodology. Because project management methodology is a critical part of OPM methodology, OPAs should be referred to rather than recreated or excluded. For example, human resource management activities should reference organizational human resource policies, and cost management activities should specify organizational financial controls procedures (e.g., time reporting, required expenditure and disbursement reviews, accounting codes, and standard contract provisions).

◆ **Existing templates.** Templates or forms are part of the project management methodology (e.g., risk register, work breakdown structure, project schedule network diagram, and contract templates).

◆ **Organizational structure.** Organizational structure (e.g., hierarchical, matrix, etc.) and culture (e.g., efficiency-focused, risk-focused, customer-focused, etc.) should shape the development of the methodology and corporate culture.

◆ **Organizational context or environment.** Consider organizational context and environment. Examples include:

- Regulated environment,
- Government agency or nongovernment organization,
- Predictive approach vs. iterative/incremental (agile),
- International, regional, or local market,
- Developing economy/market,
- Internal vs. external customers,
- Timing of capital infusion (early or late),
- New product development, and
- Tangible vs. intangible end product.

X4.5 IDENTIFY CONSTRAINTS

Identify the constraints to the project types. Constraints are those items that are required to be followed without exception. Examples include regulations and laws including environmental, reporting, or safety.

X4.6 IDENTIFY RESOURCES

Identify the resources available to assist with the development of the methodology.

◆ Identify any existing project management methodologies that can be modified to support additional project types. Leveraging existing methodologies may be beneficial depending on the magnitude of differences between project types. Characterize the differences between project types and consider those differences when using an existing methodology as a basis for developing a new project methodology.

◆ Identify relevant published guidance found in the *PMBOK® Guide*, other PMI standards, other publications, templates, or existing methodologies. These standards and other documents can provide foundational guidance that may be customized to fit the specific requirements of the organization and its projects based on the other input.

X4.7 DEVELOP AND DOCUMENT THE METHODOLOGY

When developing a tailored methodology, ensure that the action plan considers inputs, constraints, and resources. Each organization should have a procedure for developing and documenting methodology (indicated by the center box in the ICOR diagram shown in Figure X4-1). The following is an example of a process to develop a methodology:

◆ Assemble a multidisciplinary team that includes representation from key stakeholder functions in the organization that will be responsible for developing, supporting, and executing organizational project management processes.

◆ Lay out the life cycle for the type of project.

- ◆ Map out the steps needed for each phase of the life cycle. A flowchart that includes responsibilities is recommended.

- ◆ Identify the business areas that are affected by each of the steps in the life cycle.

- ◆ Determine any modifications needed to the existing business or project processes. If it is a new process, begin with the documented current state.

- ◆ Review the Project Management Process Group Knowledge Area Mapping (see Table 1-4 of the *PMBOK® Guide* [8] and determine which processes are required for each phase. Consider other resources, as applicable.

- ◆ Document each of the *PMBOK® Guide* processes with regard to how they can be tailored to fit within the organization's existing processes, standards, and requirements. Examples include:

  - *Development of a communications management plan.* The communications management plan for large organizations will need to be more formal than small organizations. In a regulated environment, reporting to government agencies may be required.

  - *Development of the procurement management plan.* Determine whether the entire project will be developed in-house or whether contracted services will be used.

  - *Development of the scope management plan.* Document how the scope of the project will be defined, validated, and controlled.

  - *Development of stakeholder management plan.* Develop the appropriate strategies to manage and engage the stakeholders throughout the project life cycle.

- ◆ Create required templates or checklists to document the necessary steps for the organization and corresponding industry.

- ◆ Document the methodology. This is the organization's tailored methodology based on the *PMBOK® Guide* [8]. Be sure to consider the level of flexibility (i.e., mandatory or nonmandatory) for each process step.

X4.8 DERIVE OUTPUT

The output of this process is the documented, tailored methodology ready for application to the project type identified.

X4.9 CONDUCT CONTINUOUS IMPROVEMENT

Organizations evolve and environmental factors change. It is important to periodically reassess and update this methodology.

X4.10 MONITOR KEY PERFORMANCE INDICATORS

Key performance indicators may be comprised of a varied set of metrics to assess the effectiveness, influence, and maturity of the project management methodology. See Section 5.8 for examples of KPIs used in project management methodology.

X4.11 REPEAT FOR EACH OF THE DIFFERENT TYPES OF PROJECTS

Repeat these steps (Sections X4.4 through X4.10) for all of the different project types using the first one as a basis for the others.

X4.12 SUMMARY

X4.12.1 DEVELOPING A TAILORED PROJECT MANAGEMENT METHODOLOGY

◆ Identify the inputs that the organization gathered during the assessment phase. These include any current practices, methodologies, and processes that you may already have.

◆ Identify any constraints that the organization is required to operate under, whether required or agreed upon.

◆ Document the organization's types of projects; if only one type is identified, make sure the methodology is scalable to the size, complexity, risk, and other factors the organization chooses.

APPENDIX X5
ORGANIZATIONAL ENABLERS FOR OPM

When implementing organizational project management (OPM), organizations need to establish a supporting environment that encourages, fosters, and sustains transformational change while supporting the more technical aspects of project, program and portfolio management. These supporting capabilities are termed organizational enablers (OEs). OEs are structural, cultural, technological and human resource practices that can be leveraged to support the implementation of best practices in projects, programs, and portfolios in support of strategic goals. Organizational enablers are foundational capabilities that are instrumental in assuring the OPM principles listed in Section 1.3.1 of this standard.

A listing of organizational enablers identified by the (*OPM3®*) [10] is provided below as well as sections of this standard that support these topics:

◆ Benchmarking—Section 5.5

◆ Competency management—Sections 1.7, 3.4, 4.4, 5.6

◆ Governance—Sections 3.1, 3.5, 4.5, 5.3

◆ Individual performance appraisal—Section 4.4.3

◆ Knowledge management and PMIS—Sections 3.1, 3.3, 4.3, 5.3.3

◆ Management systems—Section 4.5

◆ OPM communities—Section 4.4.2.3

◆ OPM methodologies—Sections 3.1, 3.2, 4.2

◆ OPM policy and vision—Sections 3.5, 4.5, 5.1, 5.2, 5.6, 5.7

◆ OPM practices—Sections 1.3.3, 1.6.1

◆ OPM techniques—Section 1.6

◆ Organizational structures—Sections 1.3, 1.6, 4.5.1

◆ Project management metrics—Sections 2.3, 2.4, 4.3.5, 5.6, 5.8, 6.2

◆ Project management training—Sections 3.4, 4.3

◆ Project success criteria—Sections 4.2, 5.8, 5.9

◆ Resource allocation—Sections 1.3, 2.2

◆ Project sponsorship—Sections 1.3.2, 1.7, 4.5

◆ Strategic alignment—Sections 1.6, 5.2

REFERENCES

[1]   Project Management Institute. 2016. *Governance of Projects, Programs, and Portfolios: A Practice Guide.* Newtown Square, PA: Author.

[2]   Project Management Institute. 2014. *PMI Thought Leadership Series Report: Spotlight on Success—Developing Talent for Strategic Impact.* Available from http://www.pmi.org

[3]   Project Management Institute. 2013. *PMI's Pulse of the Profession® In-Depth Report: The Competitive Advantage of Effective Talent Management.* Available from http://www.pmi.org

[4]   Project Management Institute. 2017. *Project Manager Competency Development Framework* – Third Edition. Newtown Square, PA: Author.

[5]   Project Management Institute. 2017. *The Standard for Program Management* – Fourth Edition. Newtown Square, PA: Author.

[6]   Project Management Institute. 2013. *Managing Change in Organizations: A Practice Guide.* Newtown Square, PA: Author.

[7]   Project Management Institute. 2017. *The PMI Guide to Business Analysis.* Newtown Square, PA: Author.

[8]   Project Management Institute. 2017. *A Guide to the Project Management Body of Knowledge (PMBOK® Guide)* – Sixth Edition. Newtown Square, PA: Author.

[9]   Project Management Institute. 2014. *Navigating* Complexity*: A Practice Guide.* Newtown Square, PA: Author.

[10]   Project Management Institute. 2013. *Organizational Project Management Maturity Model (OPM3®).* Newtown Square, PA: Author.

GLOSSARY

Capability. A specific competency that an organization needs to have in order to implement and sustain OPM.

Methodology. A system of practices, techniques, procedures, and rules used by those who work in a discipline.

Organization. An entity that may include all levels of the enterprise and may transcend business lines or divisions, including any area/business unit that has impact, influence, or involvement in project and business operations. The boundaries of an organization appropriate for OPM could vary by organization based on factors such as culture, size, maturity, and business needs. The principle is to include all aspects of project operations within an integrated framework.

Organizational Enabler. A structural, cultural, technological, or human-resource practice that the performing organization can use to achieve strategic objectives. See also *organizational project management*.

Organizational Process Assets (OPAs). Plans, processes, policies, procedures, and knowledge bases specific to and used by the performing organization.

Organizational Project Management (OPM). A framework in which portfolio, program, and project management are integrated with organizational enablers in order to achieve strategic objectives. See also *organizational enabler*.

Organizational Project Management Maturity (OPM Maturity). The level of an organization's ability to deliver the desired strategic outcomes in a predictable, controllable, and reliable manner.

Organizational Project Management Methodology (OPM Methodology). A system of practices, techniques, procedures, and rules used by those who work in OPM. Project management methodology is a subset of OPM methodology.

Portfolio. Projects, programs, subsidiary portfolios, and operations managed as a group to achieve strategic objectives. See also *program* and *project*.

Portfolio Management. The centralized management of one or more portfolios to achieve strategic objectives. See also *program management* and *project management*.

Program. Related projects, subsidiary programs, and program activities managed in a coordinated manner to obtain benefits not available from managing them individually.

Program Management. The application of knowledge, skills, and principles to a program to achieve the program objectives and to obtain benefits and control not available by managing program components individually. See also *portfolio management* and *project management*.

Program Management Office. A management structure that standardizes the program-related governance processes and facilitates the sharing of resources, methodologies, tools, and techniques. See also *project management office*.

Project. A temporary endeavor undertaken to create a unique product, service, or result. See also *portfolio* and *program*.

Project Management. The application of knowledge, skills, tools, and techniques to project activities to meet the project requirements. See also *portfolio management* and p*rogram management*.

Project Management Methodology. A system of practices, techniques, procedures, and rules used by those who work in portfolios, programs, and projects. Project management methodology is a subset of OPM methodology.

Project Management Office (PMO). A management structure that standardizes the program-related governance processes and facilitates the sharing of resources, methodologies, tools, and techniques. See also *program management office*.

Sponsor. An individual or a group that provides resources and support for the project, program, or portfolio, and is accountable for enabling success. See also *stakeholder*.

Stakeholder. An individual, group, or organization that may affect, be affected by, or perceive itself to be affected by a decision, activity, or outcome of a project, program, or portfolio. See also *sponsor*.

Sustainability. A characteristic of a process or state that can be maintained indefinitely.

INDEX

Competency framework, 22
Continuous improvement, OPM, 12, 29
Culture, 33

D

Development, professional, 32
Documentation, 30

E

Enterprise project management office (EPMO), 6, 8,
    13, 42–43
Experiential learning, 33–34

F

Formal learning, 34
Foundational concepts, 2
    investment as, 15–16
    in maturity models, 48
    OPM business case as, 16–18
    value as, 15–16
Framework, OPM, 7, 19–22
    knowledge management element of, 19, 20–21,
        29–32
    for OPM approach, 7–9
    OPM business case for, 16
    OPM governance element of, 19, 22–23, 35–37
    OPM methodologies element of, 19, 20, 25–28
    organizational strategy of, 7–8
    within organizations, 25–37
    talent management element of, 19, 21–22, 32–35
Future state, 46

G

Governance, OPM, 20, 22, 35
    entities of, 37
    EPMO and, 13
    factors assessed by, 37
    hierarchy, 36
    levels of, 36
    as OPM framework element, 19, 22–23, 35–37
    PMO and, 13
    steering committees for, 36

I

Implementation, 2, 5, 12
    business impact metric from, 56
    KPIs for, 51–53
    maturity models for, 48–50
    OPM business case development for, 44–46
    OPM initiative definition for, 39–40
    OPM maturity for, 46–48
    performance metrics for, 51–53
    planning considerations for, 54
    PMO supporting, 42–43
    process management for, 50–51
    program manager for, 43
    program organization defined for, 40–44
    roles defined for, 40–44
    sponsor, 42
Improved performance, 29
Improvement, 33
Individual learning, 30
Informal learning, 34
Initial OPM maturity level, 47
Initiating committee, 42
Initiative, OPM
    definition of, 39–40
    maturity models role in, 48–50
    planning considerations for, 54
    steps for, 40
Integration, 29, 43
Integrator, OPM, 43–44
Investment, 9, 15–16. *See also* Return on investment

J

Job roles, 34–35, 40–44

K

Key performance indicators (KPIs), 17, 51–53
Knowledge competence, 21
Knowledge content update, 31
Knowledge management
    impact measurement of, 32
    learning environment for, 31–32
    life cycle, 30–31
    as OPM framework element, 19, 20–21, 29–32

ROI. *See* Return on investment

Roles
    additional, 44
    for implementation, 40–44
    job, 34–35
    of maturity models, 48–50

S

Sponsor, 42, 86
Sponsorship, OPM, 17
Stakeholder, 1, 14, 41, 86
Strategic alignment, 57
Strategic objectives, 6, 15
Strategy, 3, 6, 9. *See also* Organizational strategy
Sustainability, 86. *See also* Benefits sustainment

T

Talent management, 21, 32
    application factors for, 32–33
    assessment for, 32–33
    competence aspects regarding, 21–22
    competency development plans for, 33–34
    job roles for, 34–35
    as OPM framework element, 19, 21–22, 32–35

V

Value
    business, 16
    creation, 15–16
    organizational, 45
    proposition, 17